MAKING
CLASSIC ENGLISH
FURNITURE

A MODERN APPROACH TO TRADITIONAL CABINETMAKING

MAKING CLASSIC ENGLISH FURNITURE

A MODERN APPROACH TO TRADITIONAL CABINETMAKING

PAUL RICHARDSON

Guild of Master Craftsman Publications Ltd

First published 2000 by
Guild of Master Craftsman Publications Ltd,
166 High Street, Lewes,
East Sussex, BN7 1XU

ISBN 1 86108 153 7
A catalogue record of this book is available from the British Library

Design concept by Ivan Dodd
Designed by Edward Le Froy
Cover design by Guild of Master Craftsman Publications Design Studio
Editor: Lindy Dunlop
Typefaces: Garamond, Sabon, TechGrapha

Colour origination by Viscan Graphics (Singapore)
Printed and bound by Kyodo Printing (Singapore) under the supervision
of MRM Graphics, Winslow, Buckinghamshire, UK

This book is dedicated to my wife Christine, and our children Amy and Edward, for their support, encouragement and often forbearance — qualities required of the families of both cabinetmakers and authors, therefore doubly so in my case.

ACKNOWLEDGEMENTS

The author and publishers gratefully acknowledge and credit the following people for their work:

Photographers

Contents photo
Paul Richardson

Chapter 1
Paul Richardson: Chapter 1 opener
Dennis Bunn: photo on page 3
Anthony Bailey: photo on page 5
Brian Osborne: photo on page 7

Chapter 2
Paul Richardson: Chapter 2 opener, Figs 2.1–2.3, 2.6, 2.15–2.17, 2.23
Anthony Bailey: Figs 2.4, 2.5, 2.7–2.9, 2.14, 2.18–2.22, 2.24–2.27, 2.29, 2.30
Chris Skarbon: Figs 2.10–2.13

Chapter 3
All photos by Paul Richardson

Chapter 4
Dennis Bunn: Chapter 4 opener, Figs 4.1, 4.28
Anthony Bailey: Figs 4.2–4.6, photos on page 58, Figs 4.7–4.15, 4.17–4.27, 4.29, 4.30, photos on pages 70, 71
Paul Richardson: Fig 4.16

Chapter 5
Chris Skarbon: photos on pages 75, 76, 78, 79, 84, 88, 95
Paul Richardson: photos on pages 77, 80, 81, 83, 85, 86, 89, 91, 92
Anthony Bailey: photos on pages 87, 90, 93, 94

Chapter 6
Paul Richardson: photo on page 105
Anthony Bailey: all other photos

Chapter 7
All photos by Dennis Bunn

Chapter 8
All photos by Chris Skarbon

Chapter 9
Chris Skarbon: photos on pages 157, 158, 162, 163, 164, 165, 166, 169

Anthony Bailey: photos on pages 160, 167

Author photo
Christine Richardson

Illustrators

Chapter 2
Paul Richardson: Fig 2.28

Chapter 3
Simon Rodway: Figs 3.2, 3.5
Paul Richardson: Figs 3.3, 3.12

Chapter 4
Simon Rodway: illustration on page 54
Paul Richardson: illustration on page 71

Projects contents
All illustrations by Ian Hall

Chapter 5
Ian Hall: illustration on page 74
Simon Rodway: illustration on page 82
Paul Richardson: all plan drawings

Chapter 6
Ian Hall: illustration on page 100
Simon Rodway: plan drawing on page 112
Paul Richardson: plan drawings on pages 113–115

Chapter 7
Ian Hall: illustrations on pages 116, 122
Paul Richardson: illustrations on pages 123, 126, all plan drawings

Chapter 8
Ian Hall: illustration on page 134
Paul Richardson: illustration on page 144, plan drawings on pages 150–55
Simon Rodway: plan drawing on page 149

Chapter 9
Ian Hall: illustration on page 156
Paul Richardson: all plan drawings

MEASUREMENTS

Readers should be aware that where metric dimensions have been converted to imperial and vice versa, rounding to the nearest conventional increment has been adopted. Where an exact dimension is critical no conversion has been given.

DRAWINGS

When making furniture, many parts are cut to fit the structure during the course of construction in order to achieve the best possible fit, and therefore, the measured drawings should be used as a reference guide only. For this reason no cutting lists are given.

SAFETY

Woodworking is an inherently dangerous pursuit. This book is intended for those who are already skilled and experienced in furniture-making, and therefore no specific safety advice is given. Novices should not attempt the procedures described herein without seeking training and information on the safe use of tools and machines, and all readers should observe current safety legislation.

CONTENTS

Chapter one
INTRODUCTION

Why, at the end of the twentieth century, would anyone write a book about making furniture in the style of the seventeenth and eighteenth centuries? Surely everything that there is to say on the subject has been said, and the real business of makers is to move forward, exploring new forms?

As with icebergs, seven-eighths of furniture-making exists below the surface – its visible, public face is almost entirely concerned with the latest, the new, the bold and innovative structures that emerge from those who refer to themselves as designers rather than craftsmen. This may be how it should be, but it does tend to obscure the fact that the vast majority of makers are working within a traditional idiom.

That they are is not surprising. Most homes are furnished in a more-or-less traditional fashion after all, and as people don't change their furniture very often, the influence of fashion is less significant than in other areas. Moreover, there is a great love of classical design, by which we mean that dating from the classical revival of the eighteenth century, and rightly so: it represents a pinnacle of man's achievement in the arts and crafts.

Whether this love of the classical in art, architecture and music is a tyranny we need not discuss – we are dealing here with what is, not what should be, and both the innovators and classicists in those fields are quite vocal enough not to need my contribution to their argument. In contrast to the modernists, though, exponents of classical furniture are a modest and silent group who seem content to merely get on with what they do. I can't blame them for that, but it has led to development in their craft being neglected in published work, and ironically, to a reversion to an oral tradition of passing on techniques.

The design and making of furniture is not a series of isolated incidents, each one beginning and ending without reference to the one before or relevance for those to come; it is a continuous process of development. The making of classical furniture is far from a reiteration of old ways: on the contrary, it is a field of great innovation. Imagine how the Georgian craftsman, used to working with the limited range of equipment, materials and techniques available to him, would react to being freed from the drudgery of propelling every tool by hand, to the possibilities presented by powerful and versatile adhesives and stable man-made materials?

Don't make the mistake of thinking that these crafts-men were reactionaries who jealously guarded tradition, as all the evidence points to their being practical and inventive, ready to adopt new techniques with enthusiasm. Let us consider an example.

A momentous change in furniture-making occurred in the early 1700s as a result of two unconnected circumstances. First, the availability of walnut, which till then had been the standard material for fine work, became much reduced due to a walnut wood famine in France which prompted an embargo on its export in 1720. At the same time, a previously rare timber became more available as it was newly imported from the American colonies, initially as ballast in the otherwise empty holds of ships on their homeward journeys. This was mahogany, and while it shared some characteristics with the then scarce walnut, the craftsmen of the period were quick to see and exploit its unique qualities.

One of these qualities was colour. We are accustomed to the pale straw colour of antique mahogany, but when these pieces were made they were a rich, deep red, which appealed to the more flamboyant tastes then emerging. This timber's stability, strength, durability

and resistance to insect attack certainly eclipsed that of walnut and allowed makers to use it in the solid rather than as a veneer over oak. Mahogany was also available in wide boards, and its hardness made it especially suitable for crisp carvings.

The result? Chairs and other small pieces became finer, with narrower components, and highly detailed carving appeared, cut directly into the structure instead of being applied separately. Huge bookcases with prodigious load-bearing capability were made, featuring intricate mouldings. Dining tables increased in size, and while the gate-leg table, suited to oak and walnut, persisted, other forms with larger, highly polished surfaces became possible.

The point of this is not only that craftsmen adopted a new material and developed the techniques it required, but they capitalized on it to develop and refine the furniture they made.

Over the 150 years following this, as the industrial revolution took place, many new ways of working were introduced and incorporated. Throughout this period there was little divergence between furniture as domestic element, as a practical craft and as a designed product.

Around the beginning of the twentieth century, however, these three elements seemed to part company. The last overt manifestation of the process of evolution described above was perhaps what is now known as Edwardian Sheraton, being an application of state-of-the-art techniques, equipment and materials to the classical form. At the same time, the Arts and Crafts movement was gathering pace and, driven by William Morris, decorative crafts became caught up in a philosophical movement that eschewed anything with the taint of industry. A number of workshops came into being, some grouped around the Cotswolds, which were operated by individuals seeking enlightenment through lifestyle; they made attractive furniture by hand process, deliberately avoiding artifice and choosing instead revealed construction and native timbers. Much has been written about this movement and it is, indeed, fascinating, but it is sometimes overlooked that many of the exponents were able to fund their work through private incomes, and I know of none that made a realistic living. It is a shame, then, that they are the examples most often held up for young craft-oriented makers to follow.

While craft was becoming confused with philosophy in this way, design took off in a number of directions. This period was undoubtedly important, exciting and valuable, and I will not attempt to even scratch the surface of a description or analysis of all its facets; its significance in our context is how it affected the making of furniture. The architect Charles Rennie Mackintosh did not restrict himself to furniture, for example, but designed some of the most influential pieces of this century. Who made them, though? Various subcontracted makers realized Mackintosh's designs, with varying degrees of success, and while original examples attract high sums at auction, they are widely accepted to be poorly made, and rarely safe to use. Quite clearly, craft had no significance in this furniture and was entirely subordinate to design.

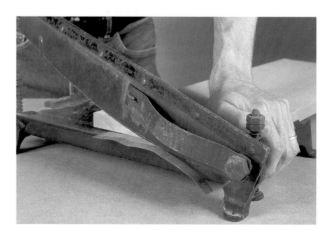

The rest of the twentieth century has continued in much the same way; craft moving in the same direction as art, and design being its own justification. Who has made the furniture that people use? On one level manufacturing industry has satisfied demand, with sound but bland furniture that neither offends nor excites. Fashion furniture comes and goes with other prevailing trends. Perhaps it is not a coincidence that antique furniture has steadily increased in popularity.

While all this has been going on, though, the thread of development has continued uninterrupted, albeit out of sight in the seven-eighths of furniture-making referred to earlier. Classical pieces have continued to be made by much the same type of individual who made them during the seventeenth, eighteenth and nineteenth centuries, and new techniques have continued to be adopted alongside the old.

This book, then, is an attempt to make visible some of the approaches that are being used to make classical furniture today. I have learned these in the practice and through an oral tradition which I have tried to approximate here with a base of five projects. Between them these projects illustrate most of the features and problems that are encountered in making period furniture. Two core techniques which may not have been encountered by the reader, hand veneering and dovetailing, are explained in detail. Some techniques, including hand veneering, are 300 years old and virtually unchanged. Some, like dovetailing, are 300-year-old techniques performed with modern tools, and others, like biscuit jointing, are entirely new. What they have in common, I hope, is that each is the most appropriate technique for the job in hand. Used together they represent an approach that should be timeless, one of flexibility and practicality in the pursuit of a sound result.

Even those who intend to work in a modern idiom should, then, find something of use here, just as a musician who performs avant-garde works will train on the classics.

In fact, this analogy is a suitable one as it provides what is perhaps the best answer to the questions posed at the start of this introduction: few musicians expect to, or are expected to, compose the music they play, and no-one questions the joy that can be gained from playing, or listening to, a great classic piece. I rest my case.

Paul Richardson, 1999

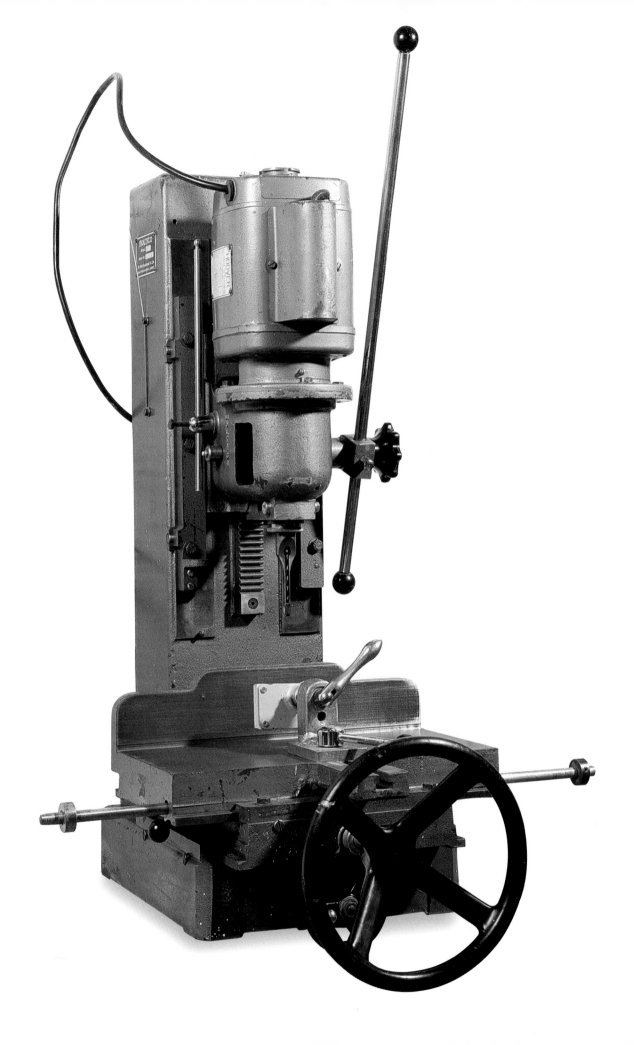

Chapter two

EQUIPMENT AND MATERIALS

This book is most assuredly *not* a beginners' guide, so I expect the reader to own and know how to use a fair collection of tools and small machines and to have a familiarity with most materials commonly available at the time of writing: indeed, the whole point is to exploit these things in the making of classic furniture.

You will, therefore, find merely passing references to equipment and materials throughout; the use of a particular machine will be indicated without a discussion of its operation or, indeed, the alternatives, and various timbers will be suggested without much background as to their particular merits.

Consequently, some discussion of these matters is required in order that we both know where we stand – but I make no claim that this is the last word on either subject, and recommend that those who wish to know more consult the wide range of books dedicated to both.

EQUIPMENT

I have never met a furniture-maker or other serious woodworker who didn't have a weakness for tools and machines, most having too many rather than too few. To successfully attempt the projects featured here, by the means described, will require no equipment that is beyond the scope of the small workshop or advanced amateur.

Hand veneering may be a special case, as few modern workshops contain those pieces of equipment that are needed, and this is covered within the relevant chapter.

Measuring and marking tools

All the tools in the world won't help if the job is not measured and marked out accurately. Many tools for marking are made of exotic timbers such as rosewood, and bound with brass. Avoid these, beautiful though they are, as all wood moves with time, and rosewood more than most. Instead, choose your measuring instruments from those offered to engineers: these will be highly accurate and, if looked after, will stay so.

Start with a couple of engineers' squares – a big one and a little one – as these will be used to set up your machines as well as to mark timber for cutting.

A 3m (10ft) tape measure is handy for boards, but don't trust it for fine measuring. Instead, use good-quality steel rulers: 1000mm (39in), 300mm (12in)

FIG 2.1

A fair selection of measuring and marking tools is a fundamental requirement

and 150mm (6in) examples will provide a good range. For transferring angles you will need a sliding bevel or two. I also recommend that you collect half a dozen each of marking and mortice gauges; they are cheap and easy to find second-hand, and having several allows all of the critical dimensions for a piece to remain set for the duration of the project.

A pair of trammel heads will be needed for striking arcs and circles, as well as finding centres, intersecting angles and so on. One final and absolutely essential measuring tool is the Vernier calliper – without one

of these to set machines and measure thicknesses, accuracy will never be attained.

Develop the habit of using a knife to mark out rather than a pencil, as sometimes the thickness of a pencil line is enough to ruin the fit of a component. It is not necessary to buy a special device – I have always favoured the ubiquitous Stanley knife.

Hand tools

A basic set of hand tools is taken for granted. Well-made hand tools are nice to own, with their wooden handles, brass ferrules and so on, but it should be borne in mind that the purpose of many of the more specialized items has been overtaken by machinery. The most unusual tool required for this kind of work is, perhaps, a shoulder plane; I get by with a common, removable-front Stanley No. 93. If you have a collector's zeal, uses can be found for almost any hand tool; if your budget and inclination lead you to minimalism, follow the old advice of buying a few of the best-quality tools rather than a lot of mediocre examples.

FIG 2.2

Excuses can always be found for buying more hand tools, but this selection represents the basic essentials

A suitable kit of hand tools might include one each of the following:

- No. 5 bench plane;
- No. 9½ block plane;
- shoulder/rebate plane such as the No. 93;
- No. 151 spokeshave;
- bevel-edged chisels in sizes from 3 to 38mm (⅛ to 1½in);
- tenon saw;
- gent's saw;
- coping saw;
- Warrington-pattern hammer; and
- Stanley knife.

Over and above these basics I own hundreds of hand tools but, realistically, those listed above are the ones without a protective layer of dust.

FIG 2.3

The Stanley Multiplane – a good example of a tool
which is nice to own but of little relevance today

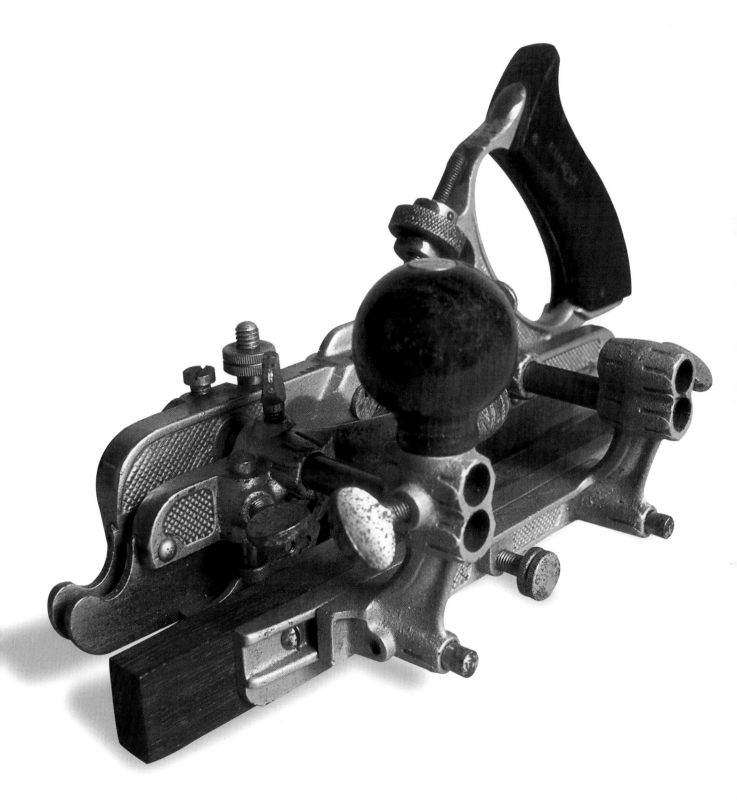

FIG 2.4 (RIGHT)

A cordless drill – one is good, three are better

FIG 2.5 (BELOW)

Hand-held circular saws are useful for cutting unwieldy pieces of timber into manageable pieces, but no more than that

FIG 2.6

A jigsaw takes care of general purpose cutting around the workshop, not just curves

Power tools

Here we leave the eighteenth century far behind, as the use of power tools epitomizes the difference in techniques available to the modern maker over our predecessors. I have little doubt, though, that the Georgian craftsman would have embraced them with enthusiasm had they been able, particularly biscuit jointers and routers, whose significance is so great that they merit their own categories below.

Powered tools began with drills, and everyone now has one, but for furniture-making, the cordless version is the more useful. Choose a light but powerful example, probably 12V, with variable speed and a clutch. You will use this constantly for drilling of all kinds, and for driving screws. Many makers, myself included, keep two or three so that we can carry out repetition drilling, countersinking and screwdriving without pausing to change their function.

A 250mm (10in), hand-held circular saw saves considerable time when rough-cutting timber into manageable lumps, and a smaller 180mm (7¼in) example will make light work of preparing 2400 x 1200mm (8 x 4ft) sheets of MDF for more precise cutting; it is rarely easy or safe to lift such a board straight on to a table saw. Beyond this though, they have little to offer the furniture-maker, as their accuracy is poor.

Modern, highly specified jigsaws are capable of great accuracy; as a general-purpose device they earn their place in all workshops. Apart from the obvious shaped cutting, a jigsaw is often the most suitable tool for trimming parts that are too large to manoeuvre over a fixed machine.

FIG 2.7

A large belt sander, the powered successor to the bench plane and good for both stock removal and sanding veneers

FIG 2.8

Because random orbital sanders leave no obvious scratches, they are the best sanders for finishing

FIG 2.9

A palm sander is handy for edges and tight corners

Sanders, for our purposes, fall into two categories: stock-removing, belt sanders, and finishing, orbital and random-orbital sanders. The former is, in many ways, the powered successor to the hand plane – power planes may be discounted entirely as their accuracy is negligible. Conversely, a 100mm (4in) belt sander is a surprisingly delicate instrument, and may be used for flush-sanding joined boards, removing machining marks and, to my mind most usefully, for sanding veneers after laying.

The heavier the machine the more stable it is, and therefore, the less likely to dig in.

Finishing sanders are to be found in all workshops. Two are required for the work featured in this book;

- a 150mm (6in) random-orbital machine, prefer-ably with a Velcro pad, for large areas; and
- a 100mm (4in) palm sander for edges, delicate components and less accessible places.

FIG 2.10

Plunge-type biscuit jointer

FIG 2.11

Swing-type biscuit jointer

BISCUIT JOINTERS

While in some ways just another power tool, the biscuit jointer is unique in that it is not merely a powered version of a traditional tool. Because of this, it has made possible different approaches to the making of furniture. Once, a good deal of a maker's time was spent on simple corner joints; now these can be despatched with speed, ease and accuracy (three of my favourite words), using this excellent tool.

All of the projects in this book make extensive use of the biscuit jointer. Two basic types are available:

- the swing type, in which the motor is mounted on a pivot and the blade is swung into the work; and
- the plunge type, in which the motor is mounted on a slide and the blade entered so that it is perpendicular to the work.

The plunge approach has become the standard, as the direct action of plunging is more positive for general biscuiting, but for grooving, scribing and trimming, the swing type has superior balance.

The 4in (102mm) tungsten-carbide-tipped (TCT) blade of a jointer has almost no run-out, so a swing jointer guided against a straightedge leaves almost as good a finish when cutting sheet material as a panel saw. To exploit this, some manufacturers offer guide rails, and fine-finish blades are available.

FIG 2.12

The action of the plunge-type biscuit jointer

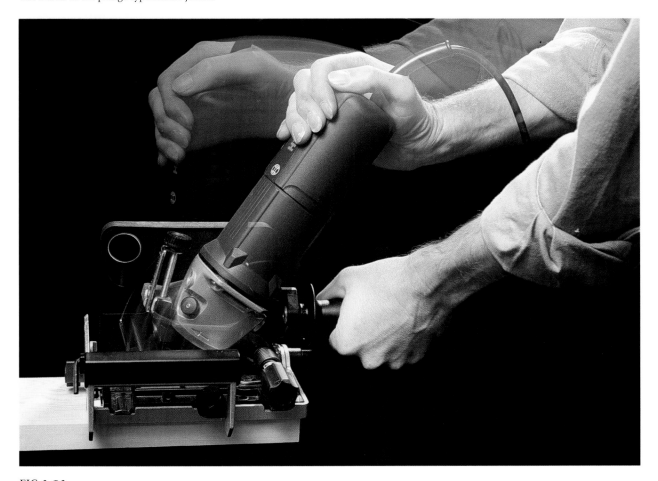

FIG 2.13

The action of the swing-type biscuit jointer

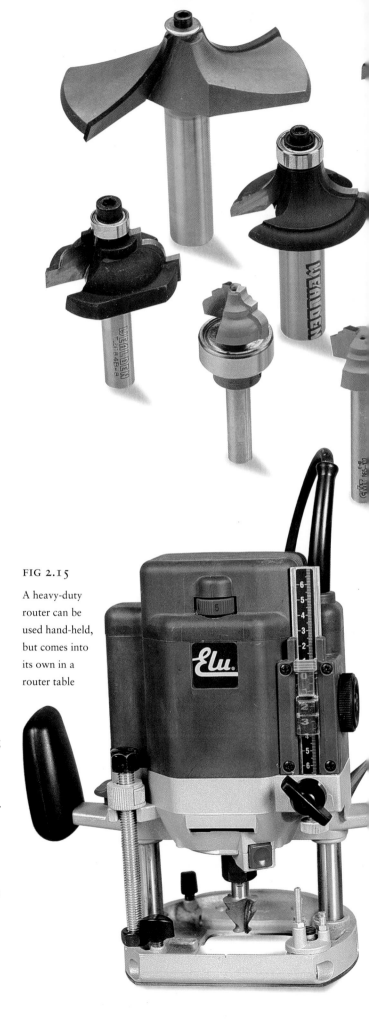

FIG 2.15

A heavy-duty router can be used hand-held, but comes into its own in a router table

Routers

If the biscuit jointer has revolutionized carcass-jointing, then the hand-held router has revolutionized almost every other technique of furniture-making. Unlike the jointer, it has done so by offering faster, more accurate and repeatable ways of performing tasks hitherto carried out with hand tools – for example, rebating, moulding and inlay work – together with some that were formerly the preserve of fixed machines such as spindle-moulders.

In short, the contemporary maker, when equipped with and skilled in the use of the router, is in a position to

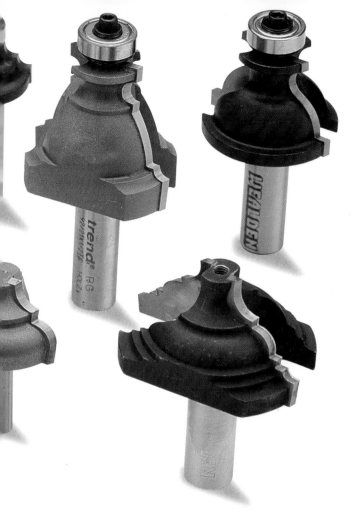

FIG 2.14

A selection of router cutters

FIG 2.16

A small, ¼in collet router for
hand-held work

execute a range of work that would formerly have
required an armoury of tools and a good deal more time.
Therefore, I urge readers who have yet to immerse themselves in the use of these noisy but indispensable tools,
to do so, and preferably before attempting any of the
projects herein, as all feature routing techniques extensively.

For the work in this book, it is best to use two
different routers: a small ¼in collet machine of
around 700–900W for light and accurate hand-held
work, and a large ½in collet router of 1800W, with
electronic speed control, for heavy-duty work and
for use in a router table.

A router table, in which the machine is mounted in an inverted position, will also be needed. This arrangement is used for much of the jointing and shaping work and for almost all of the mouldings featured, effectively rendering a spindle-moulder unnecessary. Such inversion tables are available commercially, but I prefer to make my own as, in this way, I can design it

FIG 2.17

This router table is constructed from birch ply, using biscuit joints

for precisely the kind of work that I will call upon it to do. The table pictured is suitable for all of the work featured here; it is made from birch multi-ply and constructed predominantly with biscuit joints.

FIG 2.18

Because of the superior quality of the materials used in their manufacture, there is a strong case for second-hand, industrial-quality machines for the small workshop

Fixed machines

The furniture in this book was made using relatively small machines – size is less important than accuracy and build quality. Sadly, these qualities are found less and less in new small machines: the logistics of modern manufacturing, together with the weight-sensitive issue of international freight costs, means that most are made of aluminium and fabricated steel where once cast iron and machined steel components were standard. While it is not impossible to buy satisfactory new machines, perhaps with the exception of small

table saws, it is by no means easy, and can be expensive. There is, therefore, a strong case for seeking out second-hand machines built along more industrial lines. Fortunately, machines made to these specifications are durable, and most consumable parts, such as drive belts, bearings, vulcanized tyres on drive wheels – even motors – can be replaced fairly easily. In this way the small workshop can be economically equipped with high-quality, reliable machines that can be set up accurately.

FIG 2.19

For primary timber preparation, a planer-thicknesser is needed

For the preparation of solid timber, a planer-thicknesser will certainly be needed. A suitable capacity is 250mm (10in) planing width, with a 150–200mm (6–8in) thicknessing height. Such a machine will also be useful for other tasks, such as planing tapers on legs.

As highlighted in the making of the bookcase (see Chapter 9, page 156), much cabinetwork involves the creation of boxes, the components of which

must be dimensioned precisely and cut perfectly square. For this there is no substitute for a good table saw with a sliding carriage; this will also allow for the accurate cross-cutting of parts, and for many jointing operations to be carried out. The classic cabinetmaker's table saw has a 250mm (10in) blade, this capacity being suitable for the preparation of most sizes of solid timber used in furniture.

A bandsaw takes up little floor space and is both quiet and versatile, making it a good all-purpose machine to be positioned close to the bench. Here it will make life generally easier, cutting out curved work certainly, and also straight, stopped cuts, bevel cuts, deep ripping, tenons, mitres and even dovetails. In contradiction to the comments above, several bandsaws of excellent quality are available new in the capacity range required for cabinetwork; that is, with a cutting depth of between 200 and 300mm (8 and 12in).

FIG 2.20

A table saw with a sliding carriage is a classic cabinetmaker's machine

FIG 2.21

Accurate, repeatable cross-cutting using a sliding carriage

These three machines plus a router and router table, will cope with most furniture-maker's needs. Those who make a lot of mortice-and-tenon-intensive furniture will probably need a morticer, and those who don't will appreciate one. Hollow-chisel morticers take up even less space than a bandsaw. Moreover, they can be positioned against a wall, so they offer more facility per square inch than most devices. Their usability and performance seem to be directly proportional to their weight, so look for an old, cast iron example, but take plenty of friends when you collect it.

One final comment on machines: to achieve their full potential, they must be set up carefully and kept well maintained. Here you will find the older machines more adjustable, but all will benefit from regular checks. Use an engineer's square to set fences, a straightedge to check table alignment, and remain alert to changes in motor tone and vibration, which can give an early warning of trouble ahead. Time spent working on your machines will be repaid with greater accuracy, a better finish and a more thorough understanding of their capabilities.

FIG 2.22

A good bandsaw can be bought new economically

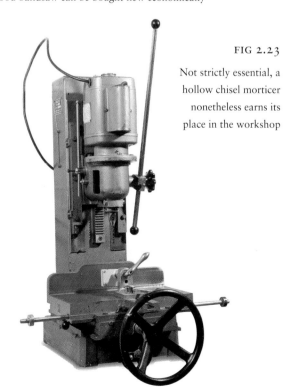

FIG 2.23

Not strictly essential, a hollow chisel morticer nonetheless earns its place in the workshop

FIG 2.24

Brazilian rosewood, now available only as a veneer, and at a cost

FIG 2.25

Solid Brazilian mahogany is becoming scarcer and more expensive

MATERIALS

Three categories of materials concern the furniture-maker: wood and wood products such as MDF, consumable items such as abrasives, glues and so on, and finishing materials such as lacquers and polishes. There is far too much to say about them for a meaningful discussion in the space available here; each is worthy of several books and indeed, many have been written. I can add little to the learned work that has already been published and will therefore restrict myself to the use of timber, and limit even this to those aspects which are especially relevant to the work in this book.

Writing on this subject at this time, the end of the twentieth century, the only real certainty seems to be an uncertain future. That this is true is evidenced by the fact that the availability and supply of some of the materials used in the making of the furniture featured here has changed even since they were made. The Brazilian rosewood (*Dalbergia nigra*) veneer used on the sofa table in Chapter 7, for example, was bought several years ago and to replace it now would

be prohibitively expensive, even if a comparable quality could be found – solid timber of the same species ceased to be available some years ago. The Brazilian mahogany (*Swietania macrophylla*) used in all of the projects but one is, at the time of writing, twice as expensive as it was when bought for the dressing table in Chapter 6, and the available sizes are fewer, as is the overall supply. Will this timber be available only as a veneer in the near future, and will even that one day be scarce? It seems likely, as this is exactly what has happened to Cuban mahogany (*Swietania mahoganii*) over the last 60 years.

Even the native oak, which we take for granted, cannot be relied upon forever. Friends in the UK forestry business tell me that this timber is being sold at a price which takes into account only the harvesting cost, and not the replacement, that is replanting, cost. It doesn't take a degree in economics to predict the eventual result.

Quite what will happen, as far as furniture-makers are concerned, I would not want to predict. What does

FIG 2.26

Quarter-sawn oak, showing ray figure

FIG 2.27

Plain-sawn oak

seem clear, however, is that our involvement with timber must become more than just a passive consumption of the stuff. A greater use of man-made boards is inevitable, and here the practice of hand-veneering will pay off. Medium Density Fibreboard (MDF) is used extensively as a groundwork for veneered carcass parts and table tops in this book's projects, and there is no reason why it could not be used for some other components.

Choices

Whatever materials are available, choose the best. The time and effort that must be invested in making a piece of furniture is considerable, and the proportionally small saving that can be made by employing mediocre timber handicaps the finished result unnecessarily.

Timber should certainly be well seasoned; preferably air-dried for at least a year before being kiln-dried to a moisture content of around 8–9%. This will rise after kilning to around 10–11%, which is a reasonable level for furniture.

References to 'quarter-sawn' timber will be encountered in the projects; this refers to the direction of the growth rings as seen on the end grain, which will be perpendicular to the face of the timber. Timber produced in this way – cut in a radial direction from the log – is the most stable in dimension and flatness, as shrinkage is greatest in the circumferal direction of what was the tree (see Fig 2.28, overleaf). Quarter-sawn stock should be chosen wherever possible, and always for such critical components as drawers. A further benefit of quarter-sawing, when using ring-porous timbers such as oak and ash, is that their pronounced medullary rays appear as figuring on the face of the boards (this effect can be seen on the mule chest, featured in Chapter 5).

Often, it will not be possible to obtain quarter-sawn stock, particularly of timbers such as maple (*Acer* sp.), walnut (*Juglans* sp.) and cherry (*Prunus* sp.). However, these show their poorest figure when quartered, so it is not the hardship it might otherwise be.

FIG 2.30

Choose harmonious timbers
when combining veneers – this
example sets mahogany
with satinwood

FIG 2.28

The effects of shrinkage on flat-sawn (tangential-sawn) and quarter-sawn (radial-sawn) timber

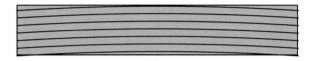

Flat-sawn (tangential-sawn) timber

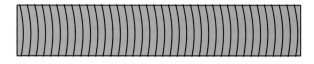

Quarter-sawn (radial-sawn) timber

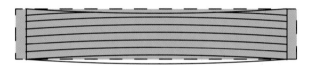

Flat-sawn timber showing
effects of shrinkage

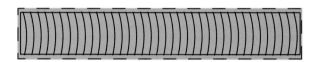

Quarter-sawn (radial-sawn) timber
showing effects of shrinkage

FIG 2.29

Walnut displays more interesting figure when not quarter-sawn

Veneers may be chosen on the basis of appearance alone, as their structure and stability is irrelevant once they are laid. The variety available is bewildering, and it is easy to get carried away by the sheer visual excitement of some exotic cuts. Try to show some moderation, as too striking a veneer can obliterate the lines of furniture. Be careful, also, to exercise restraint when using more than one veneer on a single piece – use a striking veneer along with a modest one by all means, but never use two or more spectacular veneers together.

Perhaps the best examples of restraint without plainness are seen when highly figured walnut burrs are used with plain walnut crossbanding: the difference between the two is clear but there is no clash, the plain crossbanding serving as a frame for the burr.

Chapter three
MAKING DOVETAILED DRAWERS

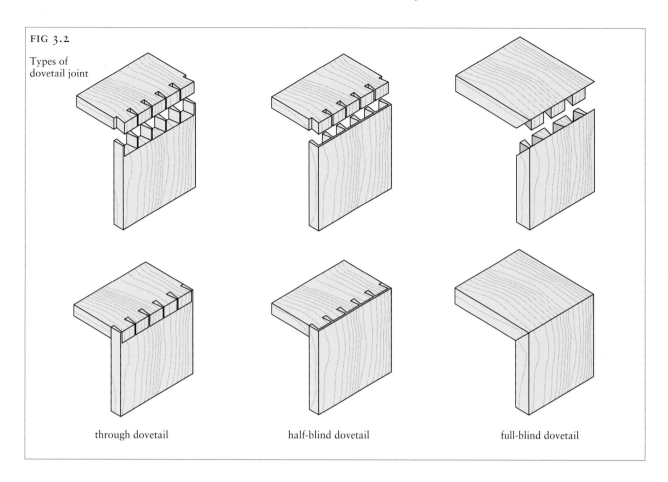

FIG 3.2

Types of
dovetail joint

through dovetail   half-blind dovetail   full-blind dovetail

All woodworkers use joints. There is a bewildering
variety from which to choose, and making the right
choice for each application is at the heart of successful
cabinetmaking. Each type has its own advantages
and disadvantages: some, like biscuit joints, are invisible
when assembled and while they resist shear and
compression stresses, they fail easily under tension
stress; others, like wedged through-tenons, have
excellent resistance to all kinds of stress but are
visually obtrusive.

Arts and Crafts furniture made this latter vice a
virtue by deliberately revealing the construction
methods used, but during the periods covered in
this book, artifice was *de rigueur*; so for the style
of furniture presented here, the concealment of
joints and other constructional features is a
fundamental requirement.

FIG 3.1

The classic drawer-making joint is the half-blind dovetail

DOVETAIL CORNER JOINTS

Much cabinet work involves the making of boxes –
carcasses and drawers are obvious examples – and
consequently, the need for a sound approach to box
corner joints asserts itself as soon as a furniture
project is considered.

Faced with this requirement, our eighteenth-century
forebears embraced the dovetail for both carcasses and
drawers. Its virtues include:

- resistance to compression and tension and to
  torsion stresses;
- resistance to shear stress in one direction (that in
  which the joint is assembled); and
- full support along wide, shallow joints without
  vulnerability to shrinkage of the construction material.

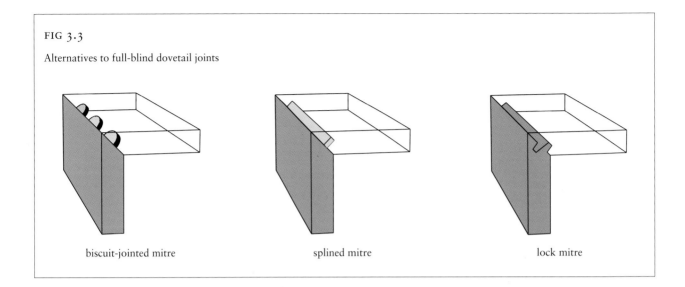

FIG 3.3

Alternatives to full-blind dovetail joints

biscuit-jointed mitre   splined mitre   lock mitre

Additionally, the dovetail is available in three levels of obtrusiveness:

- the through-dovetail may be seen on both faces of an assembled corner joint;
- the half-blind dovetail is visible on one face only; and
- the full-blind dovetail is entirely concealed once assembled (see Fig 3.2).

Not surprisingly, the level of difficulty in achieving these joints is inversely proportional to the visibility of the finished joint: through dovetails are simple, half-blind dovetails require care, and full-blind dovetails are so fiendishly difficult and long-winded to accomplish that I have never made one voluntarily.

It is fortunate, therefore, that the use of dimensionally stable, man-made boards for carcasses, together with modern high-performance adhesives, means that the need for full-blind dovetails rarely arises; biscuit joints, splined-mitre joints and routed lock-mitre joints are entirely satisfactory as substitutes (see Fig 3.3). There is, however, no substitute for the half-blind dovetail as a joint for drawer-making. Only this joint is strong enough, when the drawer sides are a mere 6mm (¼in)

thick, to resist the pulling action that is imposed on a drawer front, and nothing else would look right: indeed, many people assess the quality of a piece of furniture by looking at the exposed sides of a dovetailed drawer (see Fig 3.4).

Given the importance of a well-made drawer, this is the aspect of dovetailing that will be examined here. Equally important in period furniture is the drawer bottom, and of course the fitting and smooth operation of the drawers in their openings.

Technique

Drawers of this type feature half-blind dovetails at the front, and through dovetails at the back. Numerous jigs and gadgets are available for dovetailing with a router, but few will produce joints with correct proportions, none give a truly handmade appearance, and unless you are making a considerable number of drawers of exactly the same size – rare in this type of furniture – setting them up is time consuming.

FIG 3.4

Many people judge the quality of a piece of furniture by looking at the exposed dovetails on a drawer's side

FIG 3.5
Anatomy of a drawer

drawer slip

through-dovetails

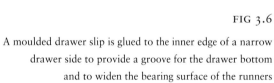

drawer bottom chamfered to
fit groove in slip

half-blind dovetails

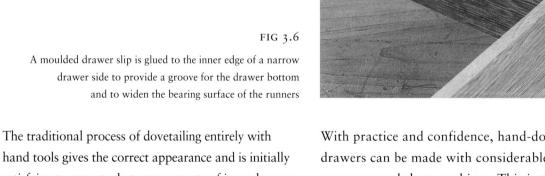

FIG 3.6

A moulded drawer slip is glued to the inner edge of a narrow
drawer side to provide a groove for the drawer bottom
and to widen the bearing surface of the runners

The traditional process of dovetailing entirely with hand tools gives the correct appearance and is initially satisfying to execute, but some aspects of it can become rather boring once the novelty has worn off, and the process can be a poor use of time. An alternative method is to use machines such as a bandsaw, to perform one or two of the more repetitive stages.

With practice and confidence, hand-dovetailed drawers can be made with considerable speed using common workshop machines. This is the method that I have described here; for those of you who *do* wish to use complex router jigs or hand tools alone, you will find these processes described in many other books.

ANATOMY OF A DRAWER

A typical, medium-sized drawer from the eighteenth century has sides and back of 6mm (¼in) thick oak and a bottom made from either oak or pine, varying in thickness from 5–10mm (³⁄₁₆–⅜in). As such thin sides will split if grooved to take the bottom, a moulded and grooved slip is applied to the bottom of their inside faces; this also increases the bearing surface that the drawer runs on, so reducing wear.

The drawer bottom is chamfered around three edges of its underside, to fit into the grooved slips, and a groove is cut in the drawer front. The bottom is fitted from the back of the drawer, sliding under the drawer's back, to which it is attached by a screw-through slot. The grain of the bottom runs from side-to-side, which means that shrinkage occurs front-to-back; thus, the slot will allow the bottom to shrink without splitting. The drawer front will be around 15mm (⅝in) thick and of a material to match that used for the carcass, for example, mahogany or walnut if solid, rosewood or satinwood veneer on a groundwork of mahogany or pine if veneered.

Drawer fronts often attract decoration; if the piece is veneered then they may be bookmatched, cross-banded and/or inlaid with stringing, and both solid and veneered fronts may feature cockbeading around their perimeter.

Of course, variations in the timbers used, in the means of fitting drawer bottoms, and in decorative treatments, are almost as numerous as pieces of furniture, and thicknesses should be adjusted proportionally for large or extremely small drawers.

TIMBER PREPARATION

Drawers that stick or rattle around in their openings make few friends. While the maker must fit them

FIG 3.7

Drawer parts are left in stick to settle

carefully, it is equally important that the timber used must be well-dried and stable. Oak for drawer sides should be selected for straightness of grain from properly dried, quarter-sawn stock and, unless bought in a thickness of around 10mm (⅜in), it must be re-sawn to this dimension and left in stick to settle for at least six weeks.

When starting a piece of furniture I first prepare the drawer parts, cross-cutting and ripping them oversize, and planing them to around 8mm (⁵⁄₁₆in) thickness. I then leave them in stick while I make the carcass and any other parts, such as drawer slips, before preparing them to their final dimensions.

The length of the drawer sides is not critical. They should take full advantage of the depth of the carcass but not be so close a fit that a stray sock falling behind the drawer prevents it from closing – 25mm (1in) less than the opening's depth is the minimum clearance to allow. The width (or height) of the sides *is* important, however. At this stage they should be dimensioned to be a tight fit in the opening. If you are making more than one drawer, check each opening; if there is any discrepancy then dimension and mark each pair of sides for its own opening.

The drawer front should be made to an exact fit in its opening in height, and a jam-fit in length; in fact, it should not be possible to insert it fully into position without force. Having dimensioned the front, cut the groove for the bottom in its inside face. This provides a reference for the slips and back, and avoids bad positioning of the front dovetails – nothing is more annoying than finding that a pin lines up with the groove.

The back should be cut to just under the length of the front – an allowance of 0.5mm (¹⁄₃₂in) is adequate. Its height is determined by the position of the bottom, derived from the front's groove, and the chosen clearance at the top.

If you are making more than one drawer, the parts for each should be marked as sets.

MARKING OUT

Set a marking gauge to the thickness of the drawer sides, then mark this dimension on the ends of the front, on the inside face only, and on both faces of the ends of the back.

FIG 3.8

Mark the thickness of the drawer sides on to the ends of the front's inside face and on the ends of the back

FIG 3.9

Mark the length of the front dovetails on the end grain of the
drawer front and on the front ends of the drawer sides

FIG 3.10

Mark a little more than the thickness of the drawer back on to the
rearward ends of the drawer sides

Next, set a marking gauge to the intended length of the
front dovetails; for a 15mm (⅝in) thick drawer front,
this should be 12.5mm (½in). Mark this dimension on
the end grain of the drawer front, gauging from its
inside face, and on both faces of the front ends of the
drawer sides.

Finally, set a marking gauge to a little more than the
thickness of the drawer back and mark this dimension
on both faces of the back ends of the drawer sides.

The next stage is to mark out the tails. The correct
angle for dovetails in hardwoods is usually given as 1:8,
but I find that this angle looks too great, and period
examples are often finer. The rule seems to be that the
earlier the piece, the greater the angle of the tails: early

Queen Anne and Georgian work often features quite
bulky, crude tails, while late Victorian and Edwardian
dovetails (sometimes called 'London pattern') are often
so fine as to result in fracture of the pins when the
timber becomes brittle with age. I prefer to work some-
where between these two extremes, using an angle of
between 1:8 and 1:10, according to the piece. Set this
angle on a sliding bevel and transfer it to the drawer
sides using a marking knife – never a pencil.

The correct spacing of tails is one of those subjects that
arouses more strength of opinion than it merits –
examine period examples and you will discover wide
variations. I work to around one pin per inch, more on
a small drawer and fewer on a large one. Thus, a
75mm (3in) drawer has either two or three tails

FIG 3.11

Transfer the tails' angle using a sliding bevel and marking knife

according to taste, and a 200mm (8in) drawer has six or seven tails, or perhaps five, because who cares? As long as it looks right and enough tails are present to be structurally effective, it does not matter.

Likewise, the size of the pins is not governed by statute. Due to the method used here, the smallest gap between dovetails must be greater than the kerf of your band-saw blade, and anything between that minimum and

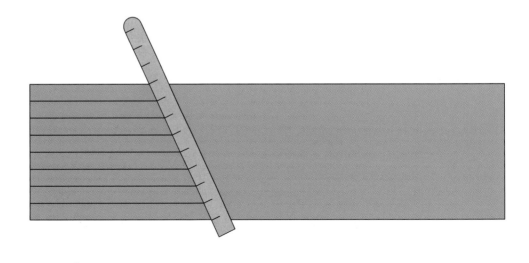

FIG 3.12

Dividing a width into equal parts using a ruler placed diagonally across

FIG 3.13

Mark the position of the back's top and bottom on to the drawer side, then mark the dovetails at an angle of around 1:6

3mm (⅛in) is acceptable. Again, this dimension should be scaled according to the piece being made; an oak chest dictates a sturdy appearance, a sofa table a more delicate one.

At each end of a row of dovetails you will find what are called 'half pins'. This is a misnomer: they should be roughly two-thirds the width of a full pin. The spacing of the pins should be more or less even, although again, it is easy to get carried away – it does not matter if they vary a little. The well-documented means of dividing a board's width into equal parts using a ruler will suffice (see Fig 3.12). Taking all of the foregoing into account, mark the front dovetails on the outer face of one side only.

After that lot, marking the back dovetails is simple. On the outer face of the side already marked with the front dovetails, mark the position of the back's top and bottom – the bottom derived from the groove in the front – then mark the dovetails at an angle of around 1:6. These are through dovetails and have little cosmetic status, so I tend to position them by eye.

FIG 3.14

Tape the drawer sides together with all edges aligned then cut the tails using the bandsaw, making each set of angled cuts first

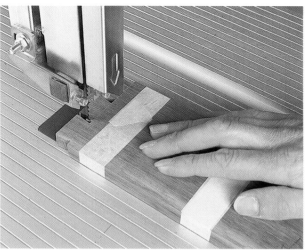

FIG 3.15

Cut back to the gauged line using the blade's leading edge as a rasp

CUTTING THE TAILS

The tails are cut on the bandsaw, which enables the cutting of several drawer sides at once. It is important that the bandsaw is set up well, with the blade exactly perpendicular to the table. Tape the drawer sides together in a stack, with the marked one uppermost, in the same orientation as they will have when made up, with their top and front edges together.

Carefully align all edges so that they are flush, then cut the tails using the bandsaw. Make each set of angled cuts first then use the blade's leading edge as a rasp to nibble back to the gauged line. A relatively new blade, with its initial sharpness taken off, works best. Cut both front and back tails in this way then clean up, if necessary, with a sharp chisel – little should be needed.

FIG 3.16

Use the side as a template for marking out the pins

FIG 3.17

Firm up the marked knife lines

FIG 3.18

Saw the sides of the pins, by holding the saw at the correct angle, from the gauged line on the end grain to that on the inner face

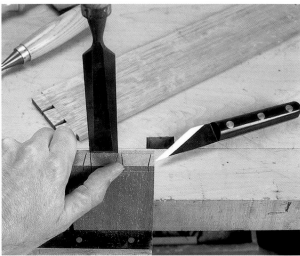

FIG 3.19

Place a chisel in the gauged line at the end of each socket and tap gently to deepen the gauging

CUTTING THE FRONT PINS

The dovetails that have been cut now serve as templates for the pins; use each set of tails for its mating component in the following process. Before starting to cut, mark the end of each component to indicate which goes with which.

The front pins are cut first. Set the drawer front vertically in a vice, with its outer face towards you. Place the mating drawer side on the front's end grain, carefully lining up the side's end grain with the front's gauged line, then mark the pins on to the end grain using a sharp marking knife. Don't press too hard initially, as the knife must follow the tails exactly; if the side is not steady enough for marking, then clamp it in position. Having marked the pins in this way, put the drawer side to one side (as it were).

You may want to 'firm up' the marked knife lines if they are faint. Be careful not to alter their position

FIG 3.20

Set a router's side fence and depth of cut, then remove the waste

at all when doing this; the best approach is to lay the knife in the full length of the marking and press until it is clearer. Hatch the areas to be removed with a pencil to avoid confusion.

FIG 3.21

Pare along the grain to finish off the sockets

Next, using a gent's or dovetail saw, carefully saw the sides of the pins, cutting exactly inside the knife-marked lines. The cut cannot be completed as the sockets are half-blind, but by holding the saw at the correct angle (see Fig 3.18), the cut can be made from the gauged line on the end grain to that on the inner face.

While the drawer side is still vertical in the vice, place a chisel in the gauged line at the end of each socket and tap gently – just enough to deepen the gauging, but not so hard as to split the timber.

If the traditional approach were being used, the next stage would be to remove as much waste as possible from the sockets using a coping saw, followed by incremental cuts with a chisel, however, a small router fitted with a two-flute straight cutter of between 3 and 6mm (⅛ and ¼in) diameter will remove almost all of the waste. To use this, clamp the drawer front face down on a bench, set the router's side fence to just under the depth of the socket, and the depth of cut to just under the length of the socket (see Fig 3.20). This restricts the cut in two directions, but you must control the length of the cut, between the pins, yourself; go steadily and don't try to remove too much at once.

This process will leave a shaving to be removed with a chisel – pare along the grain, being careful not to cut past the marked lines, although it is no bad thing for the sockets to be deeper than the thickness of the drawer sides by a whisker.

CUTTING THE BACK PINS

Cutting sockets for through-dovetails in 6mm (¼in) oak is so easy that it is quickest done by hand. Place the drawer's back vertically in the vice and mark from the sides as with the front. Cut inside the marked lines with a gent's or dovetail saw to meet the back's gauged line, then remove most of the waste with a coping saw. This will leave around 1.5mm (¹⁄₁₆in) to be trimmed back to the gauged line. Lay the piece on a scrap board and chop it back with a chisel, cutting halfway through from each face. A small triangle of material may remain at each end of the socket; this can be trimmed with a knife.

FIG 3.22

Mark the back's pins in the same way as those of the front

FIG 3.23

Make the vertical cuts using a dovetail saw

FIG 3.24

Remove most of the waste with a coping saw

FIG 3.25

Chop back to the gauged line with a chisel, cutting halfway through from each face

FIG 3.26

Trim the ends of each socket with a knife

FIG 3.27

Apply glue sparingly to both the pins and the sockets, then tap the joint together

FIG 3.28

The end grain of the pins can be lightly hammered to spread the fibres and hold the dovetails down

GLUING UP

Scotch glue is ideal for gluing dovetailed drawers, as its fast initial tack will hold the joint closed immediately it is assembled. Unless something has gone very wrong, a dovetailed drawer should not need cramping while the glue dries; just put a spot of glue on the side of each pin and tail with the wipe of a brush, then gently tap the joint together with a Warrington hammer (see Fig 3.27).

Here I disagree with received wisdom, which would have us leaving the sides proud, to be planed down later. If, instead, the drawer's back and front are cross-cut to a jam-fit as above, and we have cut the dovetail sockets a little deeper to compensate, then the *pins* will be proud instead. This means that, once the tails are tapped home, the end grain of the pins can be lightly hammered – this spreads the fibres, holding the dove-tails tightly down. Check the drawer for square before setting aside to dry.

On cleaning up, plane or sand the pins, which are proud of the sides, flush. This should result in a close fit in the width of the opening. If the drawer is made a little narrower at the back than the front, its opening and closing will be smoother.

Note that the tails at the back of the drawer project beyond the pins – this gives more support against the stress of the drawer's contents being shoved against the back in later life. The back is level with the upper surface of the drawer bottom, to allow for the bottom to slide into the slips' grooves. Glue the slips in position, being careful to align the grooves of the slips with the groove in the front and with the back of the drawer. It is more important that this alignment is correct than that of the bottoms of the slips with the sides. Ideally, the slips should be slightly proud here, to be planed flush once dry.

FIG 3.29

The slips are glued in position, aligned with the groove of the front and the drawer's back

FIG 3.30

Fit the drawers so that they run smoothly and present an even gap when closed

FITTING THE DRAWER

If the drawer front is to be veneered, carry this out next, but if a stringing line is to be added around the front's edge, this should be left until after fitting the drawer to the carcass, which is the next stage.

If the drawer has been marked out and made according to the process outlined above, it should, theoretically, be an extremely tight fit in the drawer space. In practice, it is unlikely to fit at all and must be trimmed before it can be tried in the carcass. Remove the bare minimum needed to do this – you will be reducing the height of the drawer and this should be tapered slightly from front to back anyway, so make the back fit first and then gradually remove more material until the front enters the carcass.

As with a door, there should be an even gap around the drawer front when it is closed. This should be very slight though, in the order of the thickness of a piece of paper.

Once the drawer has been fitted to your satisfaction, any stringing or cockbeading that is to decorate the edges can be carried out.

FIG 3.32
(BELOW)

Plane a shallow
bevel around the
sides and front
edges of the drawer
bottom – any
unevenness will be
revealed by the
edges being out
of parallel

FIG 3.31

Mark round the drawer bottom with a gauge

DRAWER BOTTOM

To make the bottom itself, glue up enough boards
of about 9mm (⅜in) thickness to make up the area
required and then, after belt-sanding, trim them to
a fraction less than the width measured between
the grooves of the slips. Next, cut the edge that will
locate in the drawer front exactly square to the
sides: if an out-of-square bottom is forced into a
drawer, it will distort it.

FIG 3.33

The bottom is screw-fixed to the underside of the drawer back through a slotted hole to allow shrinkage

Run a marking gauge round the bottom's edge to give a thickness of around 1mm (¹⁄₂₄in) less than the groove, and plane a shallow bevel to meet it (see Fig 3.32). An offcut of the slips can be run along the bevel to check for fit, but any unevenness will be shown up by the edges of the bevel being out of parallel. When the bevel is complete, the bottom can be slid into place and screw-fixed to the underside of the drawer back through the aforementioned slot.

FIG 3.34

The completed drawer

Chapter four
HAND VENEERING

FIG 4.1

Sideboard in Brazilian rosewood with boxwood stringing.
Veneering, especially when used with stringing, gives visual
interest to otherwise plain, flat surfaces

There was a time when cabinetmaking, as a trade, didn't exist in Britain. Furniture-making techniques were no different from those used in other areas of woodworking – primary construction, joinery and so on – so the construction of furniture was just another function of turners, joiners, carvers and upholsterers.

With the restoration of the monarchy in the mid-seventeenth century, however, came a new age of extravagance in the arts and crafts as the sombre Puritan era gave way to a self-indulgence that was to last nearly 200 years, until the Victorians rediscovered earnestness.

From the point of view of the furniture-maker, the most important aspect of this period is the introduction of veneering. This was a skill not required of turners, joiners or carvers, and so created a new class of craftsman: the cabinetmaker's craft 'was established with the introduction of veneering' as 'Veneering demands greater skill, and cabinet-making, as distinct from joiners' work, is practised by specially skilled craftsmen' (John Gloag's *Dictionary of Furniture*, rev. Clive Edwards, Unwin Hyman Ltd, 1990, London).

The extraordinary work created in the 'golden age of furniture' that was to follow in the eighteenth century would not have been possible without veneering or cabinetmakers to do it.

The real benefit of veneering is its ability to create decorative effects which are impossible using solid timbers, whether this is because the species chosen is unstable in the solid, for example burrs and highly figured crotches with a lot of short grain, or because the construction can't be achieved in solid without laminating or joining, for example a tightly curved component.

ADVANTAGES OF HAND VENEERING

As we owe the very existence of the craft to hand veneering, it's surprising that more of us don't do it. Modern work lends itself to the use of veneers, and from an environmental point of view, veneering over a groundwork of, say, MDF, makes a lot of sense.

Hand veneering with Scotch, or hide, glue is an immediate process requiring no waiting, either for subcontractors or while every clamp in the workshop is holding a caul in place. Most cabinetmakers already have much of the equipment needed, but if not, it is cheap and takes up barely any space,

COMPARISON OF ALTERNATIVE TECHNIQUES

Caul veneering

Caul veneering, whereby the veneer is clamped to the groundwork and the pressure spread by a caul similar to that used for laminating, is cheap but requires a lot of preparation.

Hot press

This is an efficient device for covering a large square footage. However, it is too large and expensive for the cabinetmaker, so is operated by a subcontractor, resulting in a loss of control over the process and in a loss of time, which is spent delivering, waiting and collecting.

Cold press

Cold presses are more affordable than hot presses, but again, they are unwieldy beasts and take up a lot of space if they are large enough to be useful.

Vacuum-bag presses

These are useful, but relatively expensive, especially if large enough to press a 10ft (3m) long table top.

regardless of the size of the work. Best of all, laying veneer by hand is controllable and reversible, so adjustments can be made during the process; this is not possible with any of the other methods. Unlike most hand processes, veneering is very quick, outpacing even a hot press for some work. The maker can, for example, veneer all six faces of a box in a single sitting. Curves present no special problems, nor do they require complicated shaped cauls to be made for every new job. Compare this with the alternative techniques listed in the table above.

But surely, as stated above, 'Veneering demands greater skill . . .'? Not in my experience. I find hanging wallpaper much more challenging! I have seen people get into a real mess with Scotch glue and veneer, though, and more workshop swearing has been provoked by this than by any other process, except maybe laminating, which is saying something. Looking at most published descriptions of the process this is not surprising, as one or two crucial stages always seem to be left out – more of these later.

BASIC PRINCIPLES

I was fortunate to be taught hand veneering in a commercial cabinet shop, where a few men produced dozens of pieces of furniture 'in the Georgian manner' every month, so their approach was of the no-nonsense variety, and well-proven.

Although some one-offs were produced there, most of the work involved small batches, maybe four or six pieces at a time, which requires a disciplined approach without needless messing around.

This suits hand veneering. The mistake most people make is to proceed carefully and thoughtfully, taking stock of progress before moving on to the next stage, just as one should with cabinet work. In fact, successful veneering must be carried out at a fair pace; stopping to think or check progress is asking for trouble. The reversible nature of Scotch glue makes it unnecessary anyway; if something hasn't quite worked it is easy enough to sort it out later.

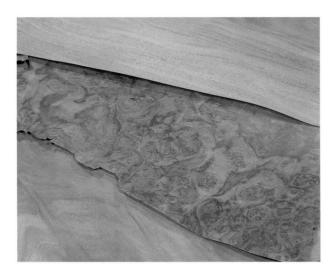

FIG 4.2

Veneering allows the decorative
use of unstable burrs
and highly figured crotches
with short grain

Heat and moisture

The two things that matter most when using Scotch
glue are heat and moisture; too little or too much of
either will cause problems. If the glue is at the correct
temperature when it comes out of the glue pot, then
it will be too cold after a minute or so – spend that
minute thinking about what to do next and it's too
late. A heated iron can be used to warm up the glue if
this happens (this will be discussed later, see page 60)
but adding dry heat in this way removes moisture,
and too little of this is as bad as too little heat.

Rather than having to deal with the problem of rapidly
chilling glue, which becomes a sticky jelly rather
than the desired liquid, simply get the veneer down
before it happens. That way, as the glue chills, it
will hold the veneer in place while it sets, and everything
works as it should.

Planning

Working quickly is all very well, but doesn't leave
any time for thinking, and cabinetmakers like to plan
their next move with the care and precision of a cat
with a mouse. The solution is to do all your thinking
before picking up the glue brush; plan exactly what
needs to be done from start to finish. Make sure that
everything you will need is within easy reach – you

won't have time to go looking for that knife halfway
through. Prepare the veneer and the groundwork
properly, see that the glue is at the right temperature
and consistency, clear your working area and take
the phone off the hook.

TOOLS AND EQUIPMENT

Hot water

Veneering, like childbirth, calls for copious amounts
of hot water on demand. If your workshop has the
luxury of running hot water then all you have to do
is turn the thermostat up, but in the more likely event
that it doesn't, a water heater is essential.

If mains water is available, then an electric water
heater can be plumbed in. This will top itself up
as water is drawn. Second-hand examples are easy
to find – if you have any trouble ask your local
electrician – but choose the largest you can fit in.
The smallest worth considering is 10l (17.5pt), but
25 or even 50l (44 or 88pt) would be better.

If, like me, mains water in your workshop is a distant
dream, then a portable unit is the only option. I'm
sure that they can be bought new, but mine cost me
the princely sum of £5 at a school fête.

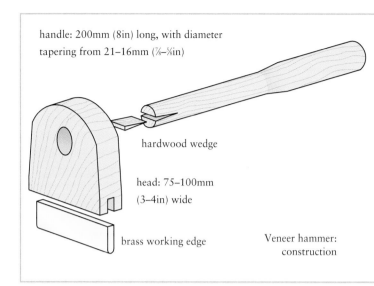

handle: 200mm (8in) long, with diameter
tapering from 21–16mm (⅞–⅝in)

hardwood wedge

head: 75–100mm
(3–4in) wide

brass working edge

Veneer hammer:
construction

VENEER HAMMER

*It is easy to make a veneer hammer
from offcuts. Wedge-tenon a handle
about 200mm (8in) long into a head
around 75mm (3in) wide, and set a
piece of brass, with its outer edge
gently rounded, into the lower edge
of the head. A 75mm (3in) brass butt
hinge, with its knuckle filed flush and
polished, can be used for this.*

FIG 4.3

Clockwise from front: Scotch (pearl) glue,
electric glue pot and Liberon double-skinned pot

To hold the water a bucket is required – this must be plastic, and with a handle (see Glue preparation, page 58) – and to apply it, a piece of worn towelling about 300mm (12in) square. Bar towels are perfect, but ask first!

Glue, pots and brushes

Not a tool, but perhaps equipment, is Scotch glue. These days most often sold in pearl form, it is diluted with water and heated for use.

Scotch glue must be kept at a suitable temperature without being subjected to direct heat, which means a proper glue pot is needed – this is the biggest investment. For very occasional use, a double-skinned pot on a hotplate is adequate, but these need some looking after as they have water between the two skins and mustn't boil dry: if this is allowed to happen, both the pot and the glue will burn and be useless.

For any serious use, a water-free, thermostatically-controlled, electric glue pot is a must, but they are more expensive.

For veneering, the glue is brushed on. I eschew the traditional wire-bound glue brush in favour of a masonry-paint brush.

Hammers and irons

To press down the veneer, a veneer 'hammer' is used. These can be bought cheaply, but are quick and easy to make (see panel, above left). A real, Warrington pattern hammer is useful for laying crossbanding. A heated iron is also needed. Older, heavy irons are best, so I rummage for second-hand examples. If you're stealing the family iron, remember that steam irons have holes in their soles and so are useless.

FIG 4.4

Clockwise from left: ancient iron, veneer hammer and Warrington pattern hammer

FIG 4.5 (BELOW)

A paper guillotine – useful
for cutting crossbanding but
not essential

FIG 4.6 (RIGHT)

Clockwise: veneer saw, old chisels, Stanley
knives, steel rule, old square, cutting
gauge and knife made from machine
hacksaw blade

Knives and cutting equipment

As will be seen later, when hand veneering, most of the trimming and cutting of joins is carried out while the veneer is wet with glue, so a knife is used. A curved veneer saw might be useful for initial preparation, but I've never used mine for veneer at all.

The good old Stanley knife is as effective a tool as any, and certainly the blades come in handy for mitring crossbanding. I use these and a knife made from a worn machine-hacksaw blade.

A luxury item for preparing crossbanding is a paper guillotine. These are in no way essential, but if you see one second-hand, pick it up.

A cutting gauge is essential, and an old square is handy. Scotch glue contains salt and there is a lot of water about when veneering, so keep a couple of old chisels (where do you buy old chisels?), say 25 and 10mm (1 and ⅜in), together with an old steel rule, for scraping off wet, gelled glue. The combination of water and salt in the glue rusts tools quickly, so it is best to use old tools for this.

GLUE PREPARATION

Scotch glue is most often sold in pearl form, which is quick and easy to prepare. Put a quantity of pearls in a non-metallic container and add cold water to more than cover the glue. Water in a metallic container picks up oxides, especially if salt is introduced, and the resultant glue will then stain any wood it is used on. When the water has been absorbed, about an hour later, put most of the now rubbery pearls into the glue pot to heat. Once the glue has liquefied, add water a little at a time until it runs from the brush in a steady stream (see below). If it hangs from the brush it is too thick and needs more water, if it breaks up into droplets it is too thin and more soaked pearl must be added.

Use fresh glue every time: once Scotch glue has hardened it loses some of its workability.

Pearl glue in soak

Judging the correct consistency

LAYING VENEER

Here I will discuss the steps involved in applying a plain veneer, in this case Brazilian mahogany (*Swietenia macrophylla*), to a groundwork without crossbanding or other sophistications (dealt with on page 64), covering just the basic 'wallpaper' technique of hammer veneering on which more complex work is built.

Preparation

First prepare the glue and the veneer (see the panels above). Soaking veneer is one of the steps least often mentioned in any written explanation of the process, but it is crucial to success. If dry veneer comes into contact with hot, wet glue, it will react in just the same way as solid woods when they come into contact with heat and moisture, expanding, twisting and buckling. Soaking the veneer in advance means that this movement takes place before it is laid, which is far better than struggling to lay a veneer while it is in the throes of changing shape!

The following steps should be undertaken as quickly as possible and in rapid succession.

VENEER PREPARATION

When hand veneering, most cutting, joining and matching is carried out as the veneer is being laid, so the only preparation needed is soaking.

Select the leaves that you intend to use and cut them well over-size. Sponge both sides of the veneer with a well wrung-out cloth soaked in near-boiling water, then put it in a stack between two pieces of chipboard or MDF. Place a weight on the top board and leave it for a while. How long veneer needs to be left under pressure varies according to its species, how it was cut and its age – a fresh mahogany veneer will need only 15 minutes or so, while an old, buckled rosewood (Dalbergia sp.) might need three or four hours. Some difficult burrs are best left overnight.

Leave each leaf between the boards until the moment it is used.

The first piece

Make sure that the groundwork is free of dust and grease, then brush a little more than half of it with glue. Quickly position the first piece of veneer on the glued surface, smoothing it down with your hand.

The next step is almost never mentioned in descriptions of hand veneering; it is to brush glue onto the top of the veneer. Why is this done? Like soaking, it encourages the veneer to behave itself in accordance with the first principle of stability: never do anything to just *one* face of a piece of wood. To offer a well-known illustration, if just one face of a board is veneered then unequal stresses will cause it to warp, so a balancing veneer is applied to the other face (though not always; see below). Similarly, when the underside of a veneer is placed onto hot, wet glue, it will buckle unless glue is also applied to the top face. In addition, veneer saturated with glue in this way will be less prone to splintering once it has dried.

LAYING THE FIRST PIECE OF VENEER

FIG 4.7
Brushing glue onto the groundwork

FIG 4.8
Applying glue to the top of the veneer

FIG 4.9
Warm the glue with an iron if necessary – keep it moving, or it will stick and burn the glue

FIG 4.10
Hammering down straight after the iron, working towards the outer edge. Note the angle of the hammer

FIG 4.11
Cleaning off surplus glue – the cloth must be hot and moist, not wet

Flattening the veneer

Having done this, apply a heated iron to re-melt any areas of glue that have chilled. On a warm day, and with an area of veneer smaller than 1m² (c. 1.2yd²), an iron probably won't be needed. If used, it should be swept quickly over the whole surface just to heat the glue, with no attempt made to press down the veneer. Be careful not to dry out the veneer or, once again, it will buckle. Too much dry heat will also evaporate the water in the glue, making it too thick to be expelled at the next stage. On no account stop moving the iron, or it will stick with disastrous consequences.

Next, take the veneer hammer and press down the veneer with considerable force, trying to squeeze out all of the glue. Of course this isn't possible, but for the veneer to stick properly, a wood-to-wood join must be achieved. Until the glue sets, the veneer will be held in place by a combination of Scotch's initial tackiness, and the partial vacuum created by expelling all air and glue.

Start in the middle and make strokes towards the edge of the veneer, keeping the hammer held at an angle (see Fig 4.10) so that the glue is squeezed out at the side nearest the edge of the veneer, in its 'wake'. Overlapping the strokes, continue until the edge is reached and the surplus glue emerges. Return to the middle and repeat the process, this time holding the hammer at the opposite angle and working out to the other side.

Quickly hammer round all four edges, all the while angling the hammer towards the outside of the veneer. If there is much glue visible on the surface, soak a cloth in water that is as hot as you can stand, and wring it out until it is almost dry. Wipe the veneer as described for the second piece, on page 61.

The second piece

Lay the second piece of veneer in the same way as the first, but overlap them by half an inch (13mm) or so. Lay a wooden straightedge along the mid-point of the overlap and knife through both thicknesses. Do this with two or three strokes; the first should be quite gentle but held firmly against the straightedge to avoid the knife following the grain, and the second or third cut should go through to the groundwork.

Now remove the waste from the top layer, then carefully peel up the top veneer and pull out the waste from below. If it has stuck firm, brush a line of hot glue along it; this will soften the glue yet hold the veneer firmly enough for the waste to be gently peeled away.

Press down the join with your hand, brush a line of hot glue over it and hammer down, this time angling the hammer towards the join, through which the surplus glue should emerge.

Wring out the cloth and wipe the entire surface quickly and firmly, being careful not to snag any of the veneer's edges. It is very important that the cloth is hot and merely moist, not wet, as adding more water at this stage is a bad idea. The aim is to just melt the unwanted glue, picking it up on the cloth as it is rubbed over the surface. Rub firmly and do not go over the veneer more than once.

Handling a cloth in very hot water is a little painful, but becomes less so with practice. Rubber gloves might help, but I find that they make me clumsy – perhaps just one on your non-dominant hand would be a good idea.

LAYING THE SECOND PIECE OF VENEER

FIG 4.12

Cutting through the overlapped join

FIG 4.13

Peeling out the surplus veneer from below the second leaf

FIG 4.14

Brush the join with glue and hammer down

FIG 4.16 (RIGHT)

Small satinwood table with crossbanding and black line. A simple piece in construction, rendered decorative by crossbanding and stringing

FIG 4.15

Clean off the glue with a hot moist cloth, then leave to dry

Removing blisters

While the veneer is still damp, catch the light on the surface, looking for the gentle bump that indicates a blister. If any are found, press them with a dry hammer that has been warmed in hot water. If this doesn't work, leave a weight on the spot, preventing it from sticking by placing a scrap of paper in between.

In fact, many blisters that are apparent while the veneer is wet vanish once the veneer and groundwork have dried, but those that remain have to be found by stealth. Brush your fingers across the dry surface, listening for a change of sound – a dry whisper. If you hear this, lightly tap the area where it occurred. You are now listening for a click, rather than the dull noise you hear when your fingers tap sound veneer. Such a click indicates a gap between the veneer and the groundwork.

Ninety-nine per cent of such dry blisters can be pressed down with a heated iron. Use just the edge of the iron and only on the area of the blister. A quick stroke should do the trick. More stubborn examples may have to be slit open with a sharp knife, filled with glue and clamped flat with a caul.

Keeping the veneer flat

According to the principle quoted above, the obverse of the panel should now be veneered to balance the stresses. I have never fully accepted this, as many pieces of antique furniture have components which are veneered on one side only yet remain flat. One answer is that these parts – table tops, carcass sides, door panels, drawer fronts – are all restrained by the furniture's construction.

However, some time ago I was shown a simple technique. If the freshly veneered component is laid face-down on sheets of newspaper until it is fully dry, it stays flat. I have no idea why this works, but work it does.

ADVANCED TECHNIQUES

Crossbanding and stringing transform veneering from a craft to an art. While both are often used to frame marquetry (in which veneers are cut to form a picture or pattern), they are more dignified when used alone to make a plain surface more interesting, without interfering with its function.

FIG 4.17

Crossbanding can be cut with a straightedge and knife

Crossbanding

Crossbanding, happily, serves both a practical and an aesthetic function.

Its practical purpose is to present a durable, end-grain edge around table tops, drawers and other parts which might be knocked or otherwise suffer damage in use. Not only is the end-grain edge of veneer much harder than its side-grain edge but, if the worst happens and a piece lifts or is chipped at an edge, only a small, easily repaired flake is damaged, rather than a long sliver as would occur with side grain.

Aesthetically, crossbanding allows the maker to define areas with a crisp and elegant frame or border, controlling the viewer's perception to either increase the prominence of details, the perimeter of a drawer, perhaps, or a frieze below a cornice, or conceal them. By crossbanding the edge of a hinged table top, as with the sofa table featured in Chapter 7, the eye is encouraged to see the top as a whole, and is distracted from the join.

The degree to which this visual trickery operates can be controlled by the strength of the contrast between the crossbanding and the main veneer. If the same material is used for both, the effect is quite subtle, if a lighter or darker toning veneer is used, for example walnut with mahogany, then a little more visual noise is introduced, and if a full contrast such as satinwood with rosewood is chosen, the effect is either striking or startling, according to the sensitivity with which it used. It is easy to go too far.

Stringing

For stringing, narrow strips or lines of veneer or inlay are used in the same way as crossbanding. When these strips are the same thickness as the veneer, stringing is applied along with the main veneer and crossbanding, if crossbanding is included; when they are used thicker than the veneer, they are inlaid into a groove or rebate that is cut after the veneer has dried. Using this technique, strings can also be inlaid into solid wood.

FIG 4.18

Alternatively, cutting crossbanding with a guillotine will give a clean-cut edge

Like crossbanding, stringing at the edge of a surface serves to protect the veneer from damage – thicker, square lines can often be found running down the arrises of a tapered leg, for example. (See the dressing table in Chapter 6.)

As a decorative device, stringing is used to define form or provide a neat interface between crossbanding and main veneers. Decorative stringing, made up of contrasting lines and sometimes crossbanding, is available commercially. A useful means of adding fine and complex decoration to a piece of furniture, it is best used in moderation.

LAYING CROSSBANDING AND STRINGING

Preparation
Crossbanding is usually laid while the main veneer is still wet. In its simplest form it is used around the edge of a panel, table top or drawer front, often with a single line of stringing between it and the main veneer.

Prepare the strips of crossbanding in advance, cutting across the veneer leaves to a width slightly greater than you need; remember to take into account the width of any stringing you plan to use. As when preparing veneers for laying with Scotch glue, sponge the leaves with scalding hot water and press them between two flat boards before cutting.

The crossbanding can be cut in any number of ways. If the leaves are kept between pieces of plywood or MDF, then a bandsaw can be used, or each piece can be cut with a straightedge and knife, using a simple jig to maintain width and parallel. Probably the best way is to use a guillotine, as this should result in a clean-cut edge and furthermore, will create no dust to interfere with adhesion.

Whichever method you choose, stack the cut pieces together to retain moisture, and press them in a vice until they are needed.

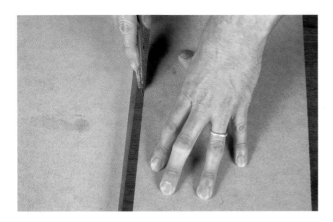

FIG 4.19

Using a straightedge and knife to trim back the main veneer

FIG 4.20

A cutting gauge can also be used to trim back the main veneer

FIG 4.21

Carefully lift away the waste and glue using a chisel

Taking a small table top as an example, first lay the main veneer as described on page 59, overlapping the area to be crossbanded but not the edge of the groundwork. Next, trim back the main veneer to leave what is effectively a wide, shallow rebate into which the crossbanding and any stringing will be fitted.

This trimming can be done with a knife and wooden straightedge, carefully measuring for width and parallel, or a cutting gauge set to the combined width of crossbanding and stringing. This latter method is the quickest and, as speed is important when veneering with Scotch glue, should be used whenever possible.

Any shaped corner other than square – radiused, for example – can be cut with a template and knife. Carefully lift away the waste and glue using a chisel, and the groundwork is ready for crossbanding.

Laying with the main veneer

As usual, working quickly is the key to success with hand veneering, so make sure everything that you will need is readily to hand. Wipe the glue brush along one side of the table top – for a larger table, work on about 1000mm (39in) at a time – then press the stringing into place. Don't worry about

FIG 4.22

Lay the first piece of crossbanding against the stringing, overhanging the corner

fitting it exactly, as this will be done with the crossbanding, but allow an overlap at each end for later trimming. Starting at one end and leaving an overhang, lay the first piece of crossbanding in place. Wipe the glue brush quickly over it, then hammer down, using the hammer diagonally so that it pushes the banding into the stringing and main veneer. Avoid fierce hammering across the grain, as this will stretch the veneer, leaving gaps when it shrinks back on drying.

Without standing back to admire the effect, lay the next piece of banding as quickly as possible, over-lapping the first. Knife through both pieces to make the join, lift out the waste and hammer back down. If you are slow the glue may gel, but a quick touch with a hot glue brush should sort this out.

Repeat this process until one side is complete, with overhang at both ends. Now start the next side, laying the stringing and the first piece of cross-banding overlapping the first side at the corner. With a sharp knife, cut through the lot to form a mitred join at the corner, then proceed along the side as before, working around the table top until it is complete. The last mitre will be trickier, as the first side's veneer will have started to dry.

FIG 4.23

Lay the second piece overlapping the first, then cut through both to make the join

FIG 4.24

Start the second side at the corner, once again overlapping the two pieces

FIG 4.25

Cut through both layers at the corner to form a mitred join

FIG 4.26

The mitred corner

Apply some hot glue to its surface to melt the glue holding it down, touching it briefly with a heated iron if absolutely necessary.

4.27

Finish all sides, then set aside to dry before trimming and crossbanding the edges

Shaped corners are approached differently, in that the crossbanding must be cut to fit from the same template as the main veneer before being laid. Likewise, bending the stringing around a tight radius can be tricky; see page 69 for details of routing square-line inlay.

FIG 4.28
Routed-in boxwood line can be used to define a simple border or create a complex pattern

Line and banding inlay

Line or stringing inlay is applied quite differently. The method given here can also be used for composite lines, which tend to be thicker than a veneer, and indeed for crossbanding when it is fitted to solid wood.

First, complete all the groundwork, including any crossbanding, allow it to dry and then clean up as usual. Next, rout a groove or rebate to take the line (see panel over page), then glue it in using PVA or similar. If you are fitting the line into a groove, the router cutter must be carefully matched to the line inlay to avoid a loose or over-tight fit; at these sizes, typically 1.6, 2.4 or 3.2mm (¹⁄₁₆, ³⁄₃₂ or ⅛in), tolerances are close, so a test cut is advisable. Note also that most suitable glues contain water and will, therefore, swell the line during application.

To fit a line to an arris, or corner, glue and then clamp it into the rebate, which may be on a curve, with masking tape.

Cleaning up

In the eighteenth century, veneered and inlaid work was cleaned up entirely with a cabinet scraper. This is still the best tool for the job and although the initial cleaning up can be done with a belt sander, and a random orbital machine will finish-sand nicely, a sharp cabinet scraper will give the best results. This is especially true with contrasting timbers – rosewood sanding dust will embed itself into boxwood line, spoiling the effect, but a scraping action keeps the colours crisp.

FIG 4.29
A line fitted to an edge is glued, then held in place with taut masking tape

FIG 4.30
Stringing should be cleaned up with a cabinet scraper to prevent dark sanding dust contaminating light timber

Tiny router cutters suitable for inlay work – the two-flute type will give a cleaner groove

A groove is routed to take a stringing line. Work in 75mm (3in) sections, moving forward and then reversing along the groove to prevent clogging

CUTTING REBATES AND GROOVES

Cutting rebates and grooves of these sizes requires special care. In the case of grooves, the angle of rotation and the low circumferal speed of these tiny cutters mean that the groove can easily become choked with waste, and to compound the problem, when routing into a previously veneered surface, the heat generated can melt the glue line. To keep things clean, use a sharp, two-flute cutter, plunging and advancing it slowly, proceeding no more than 75mm (3in) at a time before reversing the router back through the cut and forward again.

Cut the groove slightly shallower than the depth of the stringing, then run a line of PVA glue into it. Press the line gently into the groove with your fingers and then hammer it down; if the fit is correct it will be held in place without any clamping.

Cutting rebates for edge-fitted line can be done with any size of two-flute cutter. The danger here is tear out, leaving a ragged edge. This will be much reduced by back-feeding the cutter (illustrated above right).

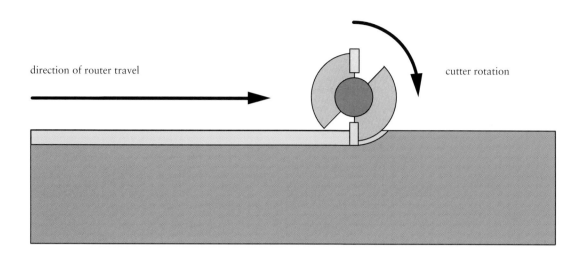

direction of router travel

cutter rotation

back-feeding the router cutter

Back-feeding the router gives a cleaner rebate for edge banding, but care must be taken as the router's travel is then in the same direction as the cutter's rotation

Apply glue to the groove, then press the stringing in firmly using a Warrington hammer

PROJECTS

OAK MULE CHEST

DRESSING TABLE

SOFA TABLE

EXTENDING TABLE

BREAKFRONT BOOKCASE

chapter five

SPECIAL FEATURES

Use of the biscuit jointer
Making broken-arch panelled doors

OAK MULE CHEST

The mule chest is a sophistication of one of furniture's most basic forms – the storage box.
The earliest chests were formed by joining six planks, and though the planks later became
panelled frames, the basic lidded box remained the fundamental storage solution for
hundreds of years. Ultimately, the successor to the box chest is the chest of drawers, but
along the way came the rather nicely balanced mule chest.

Unlike a mule chest, this piece has doors above its drawers instead of a hinged lid

Some pieces of furniture stick in my mind, lodging firmly in the 'I must get round to making one of those' section of my mental to-do list, which gets longer every day. One such piece was the relatively humble mule chest. A mule chest is a sophistication of one of furniture's most basic forms – the storage box or box chest. The earliest chests, or coffers, were formed by joining six planks – front, back, sides, bottom and top – and though the planks later became panelled frames, the basic lidded box remained the fundamental storage solution for hundreds of years.

Ultimately, the successor to the box chest is the chest of drawers, but along the way came the rather nicely balanced mule chest – a box chest sitting on top of a couple of drawers. Leaving aside practicality, I find the visual balance of framed and fielded panels above drawers with plate handles especially pleasing. Add another of my favourites, bracket feet, and some nicely figured quarter sawn oak, and a truly classic piece of English furniture results.

MODIFICATIONS

The only drawback of the mule chest is its lift-up lid. This makes it unsuitable for displaying objects on top and requires more leaning over to access the contents than most people want to be involved with. The panelled front may be converted into doors without causing visual clashing, and this allows the top to be fixed. However, such a modification does completely overturn the construction employed in a chest.

A chest need be no more than four sides joined at the corners, normally with corner posts. For doors to be fitted, a much more complicated framework must be used: unlike a solid panel, doors cannot play a structural role. Consequently, this piece borrows its construction from later styles, with the main structure comprised of the two sides, connected by horizontal parts. In this way the front has no structural implication and the back serves only to keep the carcass square.

The trick is to employ this radically different construction without it interfering with the appearance of the mule chest. Here, this is done by focusing the viewer's attention on the framed and panelled construction, with fielding and heavily figured oak, and by adding as little as possible to the exterior to suggest anything other than a seventeenth-century mule chest. Unless you are very familiar with this kind of work, it would be wise to make up a full-size drawing of the component pieces on MDF or similar

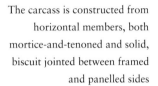

The carcass is constructed from horizontal members, both mortice-and-tenoned and solid, biscuit jointed between framed and panelled sides

before starting work. It is easier to work out the relationship of the parts with a pencil in your hand than with a saw.

TIMBER SELECTION

For traditional oak furniture, the quality of the timber used is of paramount importance. The heavy visual blocks involved must be broken up by colour, grain and texture to avoid a sombre, funereal look.

For this chest I used the best-figured oak – ironically, for such a quintessentially English chest, from France. I bought about 8 cu ft of generous 25mm (1in) thick stuff, which allowed for further selection as I made up the cutting list.

There is only one way to get a cutting list out of waney-edged English oak while obtaining the best visual effect for critical components, and that is to lay out the boards on the floor and mark out the parts with wax crayon, nesting them together to avoid wastage. At least that's how I do it when I have enough clear space on my workshop floor. When, as is more usual, things are cramped, I stand all the boards on their long edges, flipping through them like a card index. Whatever method you use, it is

worth spending time on this stage to avoid the best figure ending up on internal parts.

CONSTRUCTION

Although this is firmly a classic piece, it departs from traditional construction quite severely in places. The carcass sides and doors have, in place of mortice and tenons, tongue-and-groove joints. Tongue-and-groove joints are quite safe in this instance, as the solid panels add strength and the stiles and rails are very wide, allowing a long joint. Glue technology is so much more advanced now than in the eighteenth century that, providing the gluing area is large, mechanical strength is less important than it once was. I used a polyurethane glue throughout this chest. Polyurethane glues, such as Gorilla Glue or Titebond Polyurethane, are good performers and have the further merit of not leaving black stains on oak.

The panelled sides of the chest are held apart by jointed frames top and bottom – morticed and tenoned this time – with a solid horizontal division between the drawers and the cupboard. These three horizontal carcass members are biscuit-jointed to the sides and cut round the vertical facings, which are also biscuited to the carcass sides.

BISCUITS

The principle of biscuiting is a simple one, with a clever twist. A saw blade is plunged into two edges to be jointed, leaving a shallow kerf in each part. Because the fence of a biscuit jointer indexes on the face of the work, these kerfs are exactly the same distance from their respective faces, regardless of any difference in thickness – this makes the tool just as useful for corner joints as for edge-to-edge work.

Biscuits can also be set well away from an edge, using the tool's baseplate as a fence, to form 'T' joints for divisions within carcasses and for shelves. Once you have cut the slot, place an oval biscuit of compressed beech into the kerf, using a small quantity of glue, then glue the other kerf and bring the two parts together . . . a perfectly flush joint results.

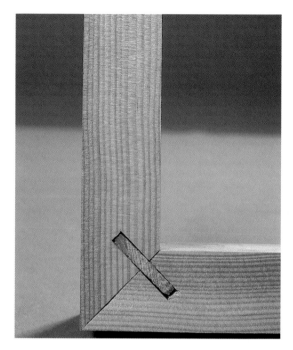

Unlike a dowel, a biscuit will move slightly along its slot to allow for alignment, so around 6mm (¼in) of tolerance in positioning is acceptable. This means that a pencil stroke

A drawer divider is biscuited in place between the bottom frame and the fixed shelf.

The back is another morticed and tenoned frame, this time grooved to take loose panels. It extends down only to the fixed shelf, leaving the back of the drawer apertures open.

The drawers themselves are as conventional as they come, hand-dovetailed as described in Chapter 3, and the bracket feet are made according to eighteenth-century norms, complete with glue blocks. To allow the feet to sit outside the vertical line of the carcass, a moulding is planted around the base. The chest's top is slot-screwed to the top carcass frame from below.

ASSEMBLING THE CARCASS

Cut all parts from the sawn boards, then plane and thickness to finished sections.

Panels, shelves and top
It is best to achieve a set of sub-assemblies as soon as possible, so the first job is to join the boards needed to make up the wide components – in this case the panels, shelves and top – with biscuit joints, but make sure the biscuits are far enough from the ends not to be revealed when cutting the panel-raise.

Sides and doors
Now the frames for the sides and doors can be made up. Remember to add an allowance to the

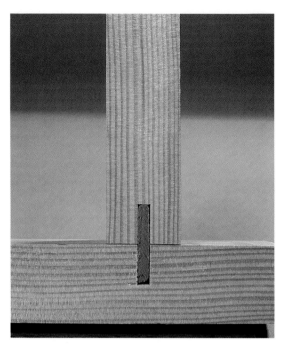

across the offered-up joint is all that is needed for marking out, and the joint can be rubbed slightly in order to spread the glue evenly and express any surplus.

The twist is that the biscuits then absorb the glue's moisture and swell. This results in a tightening of the joint which reduces the clamping time required.

width of each door's inner stile for the closing rebates (see Fig 5.2). I used a matched pair of tongue-and-groove router cutters for the jointing. They cut a 12 x 6mm (½ x ¼in) tongue on the ends of the rails, and a corresponding groove in the inner edge of the stiles and rails which takes both the rails' tongues and the dry-fitted panels.

In the absence of a purpose-made pair of cutters, these joints can be cut using wing cutters mounted on an arbor, but test cuts must be made to ensure a good fit.

Don't even think of using a hand-held router for this job – a nice flat router table with a mitre guide is essential. Cut the tongues first, then the grooves.

Leave the upper door rails square for this operation, cutting their arches (see panel on page 82) last of all before completing the groove, carefully! Before changing the cutter, groove a 150mm (6in) long piece of scrap.

Panel raising

Now for the panel raising. This is another job for the router table, but this time with a large diameter, panel-raising cutter. This must be fitted with a guide bearing for the shaped work, although the straight edges are best fielded against a fence. These cutters are *not* safe at high speeds; only use them in variable speed routers, set to the slowest speed – a maximum of 12,000rpm.

The side panel is raised and fielded, dry-fitted into a tongue-and-grooved frame. This method allows the timber to move without causing problems with cracking and distortion

Completed side member – note the rebate for the back and the relief for the skirting board. Biscuit slots for the horizontal top and bottom members are cut using the jointer's fence indexed against the ends of the side member; the slots for the middle member are cut using the base of a jointer indexed against the drawer divider, which is located for this operation by a temporarily fitted bottom member

The aim is to produce a raising with a flat tongue that fits the groove in the stiles and rails. Do this by cutting in several passes, incrementally increasing the height of the cutter as each pass is made and, as the final dimension is approached, checking for fit with the grooved piece of scrap. Test the fit all the way round each panel as the cut can vary. Make each pass across the ends of the panels first, then along the long grain, to avoid tear-out. Making two passes at each depth setting will help to even out any discrepancies.

This operation completes the square side panels, but the broken arches of the door panels need a little more work. Leave them square, but cut to width, while you field their bottoms and sides, then complete the broken arch (see panel over page).

Finish-sand the fielding and inner edges of the stiles and rails, then glue up the doors and side panels. If the rails' ends are square before assembly, it is hard to end up with and out-of-square panel, but making these assemblies a little over-size allows for final dimensioning and squaring off after they are made up.

The side panels may now be rebated for the back, and the skirting board relief, if required, can be cut.

Frames

Although a tongue-and-groove joint is used for the doors and sides, this would not be suitable for the frames which make up the top, bottom and back of the carcass. The sections of the components involved are, in relation to the overall size of the frames, much smaller, resulting in less gluing area and greater racking stresses. As a consequence, mortice and tenon joints should be used for these frames, in deference to their crucial structural role. Groove the inner edges of the back panel's frame for dry-fitted panels; these may be made up from solid oak or veneered plywood.

As before, these frames should be made a little oversize and trimmed after assembly. Note that the back panel is fixed straight onto the top frame and solid horizontal member, but it is rebated into the sides. The top and bottom frames, and the solid carcass member which forms the floor of the cupboard, project in front of the carcass sides by the thickness of the side facings (see Fig 5.3) and must be notched to accommodate them. These notches are easier to cut before the carcass is glued up, although for a better final result, leave a little to be trimmed after assembly.

BROKEN ARCHES

Broken-arch door panels are a nice feature, but the calculations can be difficult. The flat inner area of the fielded panel must be topped with a full half-circle. This means that the outer perimeter of the panel is less than a full half-circle, as is the radiused inner edge of the top rail. Because the panel is grooved into the rail, its outer radius is greater than the rail's, all of which makes a full-size drawing strongly recommended. Working from this drawing, and referring to the drawing here, first mark out and cut the shape of the top rails, finding the centre of the radius as described below.

MARKING OUT

Working on the back of the panel, draw a centre line top to bottom. Dry-assemble a door frame, then measure from the inner edge of the bottom rail to the inner edge of the shoulder of the arched top rail. Add twice the length of the tongue to this measurement to give the distance from the bottom of the panel to the cut line of the shoulder (dimension A), and mark on a line across the full width of the panel at this height.

Next, starting from the point where this line crosses the centre line drawn earlier, measure back towards the bottom of the panel, along the centre line, a distance equal to the length of the tongue plus the width of the fielding (dimension B). This gives you the centre of the various radii involved.

Now, starting again from the intersection of the shoulder-cut line and the centre line, measure towards the top of the panel, a distance equal to the height of the arch of the

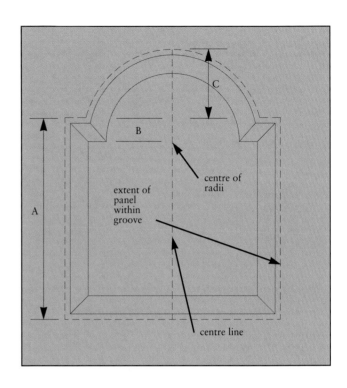

top rail (dimension C), and mark on a line at this height. With one of its points at the centre mark of the radii, set a trammel to this line and draw on the radius of the arch.

CUTTING

Cut the square shoulders first, then the radius. This latter is best done with a router guided by a trammel. When complete, clean up the internal corners with a chisel.

Now the fielding can be routed on the router table as with the straight edges, but this time using the cutter's guide bearing. This operation is quite dangerous, so use a start pin, ensure safe guarding – if necessary make a Perspex guard and fix it to the table to cover the cutter – and use temporary handles pinned to the back of each panel to feed the work. Go carefully, in shallow passes, until the correct depth is reached.

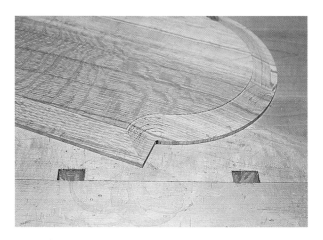

CHISEL WORK

You will notice that the cutter leaves a radiused internal corner where the internal mitre should be (see above); this can only be completed with the use of chisels.

First, define the quirk of the raised, flat part of the panel by scribing downwards with a wide chisel and paring a flat at the top of the chamfer, then doing the same for the tongue at the base of the chamfer (see above right).

To be absolutely correct, the intersection of a curved moulding with a straight moulding should be a curve, but in practice a straight mitre line is both acceptable and achievable. Scribe a straight mitre line, again with a wide chisel, from corner to corner. Don't go too

deep. Now pare the chamfer of the shoulder, working in towards the mitre. A wide chisel will do most of this, but a skewed chisel is useful to finish off. Complete this side of the mitre before proceeding (see below left).

Finish the job by paring the chamfer of the arch, again working towards the mitre, although it may be easier to make the cuts across the grain. Proceed carefully, checking progress regularly, until a clean mitre is obtained (see below).

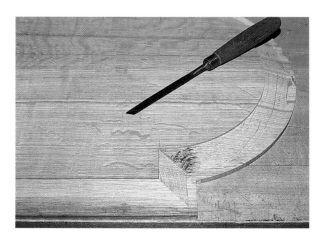

Drawer divider

Before gluing up, one more component must be prepared – the drawer divider. This is made from two pieces of oak; the main part, with grain running front-to-back, and a smaller piece, used to form a muntin rail which is biscuited to the front. The completed divider is, in turn, biscuited between the bottom frame and the solid member.

Gluing up

All three horizontal parts should now be ready for biscuiting to the sides. The top and bottom parts are straightforward corner joints cut from the biscuit jointer's fence, and the mid-panel joint for the solid member is made using the drawer divider as a guide for the biscuit jointer's baseplate.

Having cut and checked all the biscuit slots, glue and cramp as follows:

1 Make up the drawer divider, with the bottom frame and solid member as a sub-assembly, cramp and allow to dry.

2 Glue and cramp this and the top frame between the sides, paying particular attention to squareness and the lining up of front edges.

Once the carcass is dry and cleaned up, cut or trim the notches for the side facings, if you haven't already done so, then biscuit the facings to the edges of the sides. If you have a biscuit cutter for the router, it is possible to fit a biscuit across the top and bottom of the facings, inside the notches.

Clean up thoroughly, planing flush the leading edges of all parts that make up the front of the carcass, and rout a small v-groove along the join between the sides and facings to tidy it up, using a ¼in collet router with a side fence. The main structure is now complete.

The base moulding is a cove and bead, glued to the face of the carcass and mitred at the corners. To provide a secure mounting for the feet, it must be exactly flush with the bottom of the carcass

BASE MOULDING AND BRACKET FEET

Now that the basic carcass is together, the other parts can be made to fit, starting at the bottom with the bracket feet. The bracket foot is one of my favourite period details: as it is fitted slightly proud of the carcass it gives the piece an appearance of sitting firm and square on the floor, without looking as heavy as a solid plinth.

A convenient aspect of bracket feet is that they are made from 25mm (1in) timber, so if they are used, a whole piece can be made from one bought thickness.

The front feet are mitred together, those at the back are butt-joined – glue blocks are used in both cases

The drawers have heavy
proportions to suit the chest

Drawer openings; note the
kickers and drawer stops
glued in position

Before the feet can be attached though, a moulding
must be added to the base of the carcass to provide
both a visual break and an extended ledge for the
feet. The moulding itself is a cove and bead. Router
cutter suppliers call this a 'classical mould', though
I wish they wouldn't. It is mitred at the corners, and
while it can be pinned, biscuited or otherwise fixed
on, the gluing area is so large that it can be simply
glued and clamped to the base perimeter. The
moulding must be flush with the bottom of the
carcass for the feet to sit properly; it is safest to fit
it slightly proud, then plane it flush when dry.

Each front foot comprises two shaped parts, mitred
together. It is best to cut the mitres before cutting the
profile, which is bandsawn and then sanded to shape,
unless the pattern will be used again; this justifies
making a routing template for use with a bearing-
guided, flush-trimming cutter on a router table.

The two mitred parts are glued together and to the
base of the carcass, then glue blocks are added inside
the corner thus formed and to the carcass. Rubbed
joints are used throughout. Traditionally, Scotch glue
is used for this: its fast grab means that clamps are
not needed. I still use it unless the glue pot is cold, in
which case I use a fast-setting PVA such as Franklins'

Wood Moulding Glue. With either adhesive, the
parts are rubbed into position, held briefly while the
glue grabs, then left to dry. The mitre may also
be pinned through the joint if necessary; any slight
openness can be dealt with later by lightly hammering
the oak along the join.

The back feet are even easier, consisting of one
shaped piece, one plain piece butted to it, and glue
blocks along the inside of the joins.

DRAWERS

Working upwards, the next parts required are the
drawers. The openings are almost ready for them,
but require kickers to be fitted to the outer runners.
These are prepared to slightly less than the width of
the internal measurement of the side facings, and
glued in position.

The drawers themselves are the usual dovetailed
affairs. The best highly figured oak should be used
for the fronts, and plain but quartered stuff for the
sides and back. With a chest of this kind thin, fine
drawer sides look wrong and are not called for, so
they are finished thick enough to be grooved for the
bottoms. Cut the fronts just too wide – by 1mm

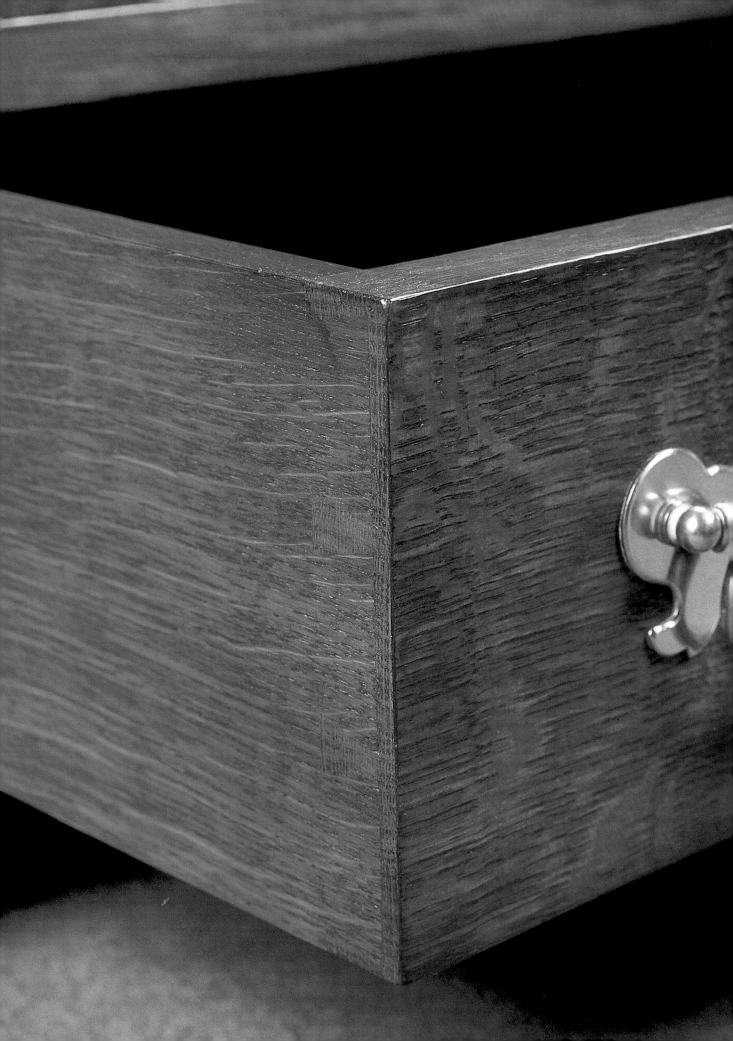

The adjustable shelf is supported by brass pegs which are concealed in recesses routed in the shelf

The thickness of the drawer sides allows them to be grooved directly for the drawer bottom, so slips are not needed

(½in) – to fit in the openings, then mark out the dovetails on the sides and cut them on the bandsaw. The shape of these is then transferred to the fronts and backs with a marking knife. Cut the sockets for the tails fractionally deeper than the thickness of the sides – more so in the backs – then glue up, hammering the pins over to pinch the dovetails closed. After cleaning up the sides, the drawers should be a near fit. Make sure that the carcass is sitting on a flat, level surface to avoid any distortion of the openings, then adjust the fit of the drawers as necessary. Finally, fit the bottoms. These slide into their grooves from the back and are screwed up, through a slot, into the drawer back.

Drawer stops can now be fitted. Allow the drawers to sit inside the carcass front a little, as this will accentuate their edges: remember, this isn't a smooth, modern piece, so every element should be clearly defined.

SHELF

The shelf is made from solid timber, and being adjustable, is not held flat by the structure. This means that it must be constructed in such a way as to allow for dimensional fluctuation due to changes in humidity, and the simplest method is to fit breadboard ends, or

cleats. These pieces, fitted across the ends, have a sliding joint which allows the shelf to move but holds it flat. To avoid the ends of the cleats being seen when the doors are opened, they should be made slightly narrower than the internal depth of the side facings.

Make up the main part of the shelf by biscuiting together boards to achieve the depth required. When these are dry, square off the ends and rout a tongue on each, then rout a corresponding groove in one edge of each cleat; the same matched tongue-and-groove cutter set as was used to make the door and side panel joints can be pressed into service for this. Glue and cramp the cleats, then trim when dry.

The shelf is supported by small brass pegs. These fit tightly into 5mm holes drilled in the carcass sides (see opposite), which provides adjustability while being unobtrusive. It is worth making a simple jig to drill the series of holes required. Jig is a strong word, actually, since all it consists of is a strip of 6mm (¼in) MDF or similar in which as many holes are drilled as desired – three, in this case. Place this jig in one corner of the carcass and drill through the holes, then do the same in the remaining three. Wear of the jig's holes isn't a problem, as each hole is used only four times and the jig is disposable.

The meeting edges of the doors
are rebated together; at the front
the right-hand door has a beaded
edge to give visual balance

The top is moulded in a
cove and bead, matching
the base moulding

The shelf can sit directly onto the pegs, but it is neater if a small recess is routed for each support as shown in the photo on the previous page.

TOP

Like all of the wide components, the top is made up of narrower boards biscuit-jointed together. The top is critical in terms of appearance, though, so it is best to use no more than two boards if possible; certainly no more than three.

It would look quite wrong to use cleats on the top, and even though it is slot-screwed to the carcass, any deflection from flat will be very noticeable, so choose the most quarter-sawn boards you have; being oak, these will be the best looking boards anyway, so they are appropriate on both counts – structural and visual. Position the biscuits carefully to avoid their being revealed when the top is trimmed to size, and take special care, when clamping, that the top is quite flat. Using sash cramps on alternate faces will help, but avoid applying too much pressure as this can cause distortion. Trim the top to size when the glue is dry.

Rout the moulding round the front and side edges of the top (note that it is a cove and bead, as with the base

moulding). With furniture of this period, by which I mean any time before the twentieth century, it is important to keep the variety of mouldings to a bare minimum – the quickest way to turn a timeless classic into a tacky reproduction is to cover it with unnecessary mouldings.

As already mentioned, the top is slot-screwed to the carcass. In fact, those screws fitted through the front rail into the top are not fitted through slotted holes: they are plain, so that any shrinkage that occurs will not reduce the overhang at the front. The screws at the middle and back are fitted through slots, allowing movement at the back only.

DOORS

Although the doors are made at the same time as the side panels for the sake of convenience, they are not progressed beyond basic assembly until this point, as they must first be fitted to the opening, with a consistent gap around them – approximately one veneer thickness all round. The doors are also rebated together at the inner edge, and this should be done before they are fitted.

The inner stiles should be 10mm (⅜in) wider than the outer stiles, and each door should be 5mm (³⁄₁₆in) wider

A till lock allows the
right-hand door to
catch against the
left-hand door

Doors, drawers and hardware
should be fitted with the carcass
on a flat, level surface – a
bench top is suitable and
presents the job at a comfortable
working height

than half the width of the door opening. This is
because the centre of the pair of doors, when they are
closed together, passes though the middle of the
rebates, giving 5mm (³⁄₁₆in) extra door width each
side. To ensure that the doors look balanced, the
door which is rebated on its inner face has a bead on
its outer face of the same width as the rebate – 10mm
(³⁄₈in) – positioned so that the centre of the pair passes
through the middle of the bead. It is easy to make a
mistake when calculating these additions and
subtractions, so draw it out full-size to double-check
before cutting.

Once the closing rebates and bead have been cut, the
doors should be fitted to the opening as a pair. Place
veneer shims all round and when the doors sit firmly
in the opening with the shims in place, the fit is
correct. If the floor isn't level at the chest's eventual
destination, the feet can be shimmed until the carcass
is square, but if you fit the doors to an out-of-square
carcass, you will have to shim the carcass to force it
into wind when you site the piece, in order to make
the doors work – bad practice.

A flat, level bench is ideal as a register surface for
this kind of fitting, and has the further advantage of
presenting the job at a comfortable working height.

HARDWARE

After fitting the brass butt hinges to the doors,
it is logical to fit the other hardware. Always fit
up before the piece is polished, ignoring the
temptation to leave it till later – even drilling
pilot holes for screws can place the finish at risk,
and often more intrusive work is required for
bolts and so on.

Door handles rarely look right on this kind of
furniture, and would be inconsistent with the
appearance of a mule chest. Effective catches
for a meeting pair of doors are hard to find too,
but both problems can be solved at one stroke
by using a till lock and flush bolts. This solution
allows for a modest wire escutcheon to be fitted,
while the key, left in the lock, functions as an
effective handle.

The flush bolts used here are, although nicely
made themselves, supplied with an unsuitable,
bent, sheet brass catching plate which is also
intended to perform the function of door stop.
As is often the case, a better solution can be found
than that envisaged by the manufacturers. Fit
the bolts. These catch in slots cut in the carcass

An oak chest based
on a seventeenth-century
mule chest

Flush bolts catch directly
into slots cut in the carcass,
holding the left-hand door
securely closed

(see photo above), which should be marked from
the bolts and cut at this stage. Stopping the doors
can be done in any one of a number of ways:

- before assembly, a rebate can be cut in the top
  rail and solid horizontal member;
- a strip can be applied top and bottom; or
- a small stop, like those used for the drawers, can
  be fitted (as was done here).

POLISHING

When all the hardware is fitted satisfactorily,
remove it so that the chest can be polished. If time
allows, it is preferable to leave the piece assembled
in the white (that is, before it is stained and polished)
for a week or two, to allow for any initial settling
and consequent necessary adjustment.

The colour of this chest is derived from vandyke
crystals, and the actual finish is a beeswax recipe.
A similar appearance can be achieved with a brown
oak grain filler, followed by a muddy French
polish, made by adding various spirit stains to
garnet. This should then be cut back with 0000
grade wire wool, then finished with button polish
and finally, a suitable coloured finishing wax.

FIG 5.1 MULE CHEST:
GENERAL ARRANGEMENT

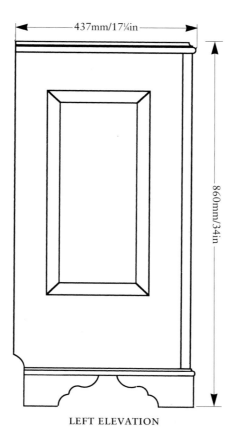

437mm/17¼in

860mm/34in

LEFT ELEVATION

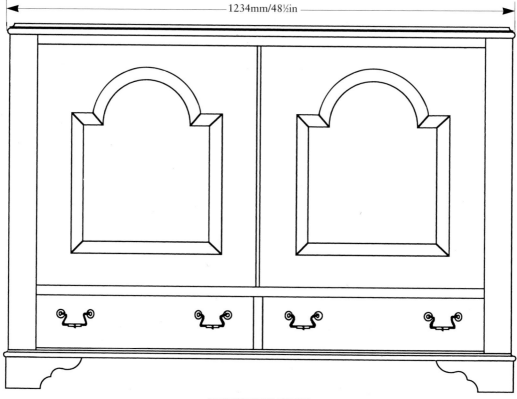

1234mm/48½in

FRONT ELEVATION

FIG 5.2 MULE CHEST: DOORS

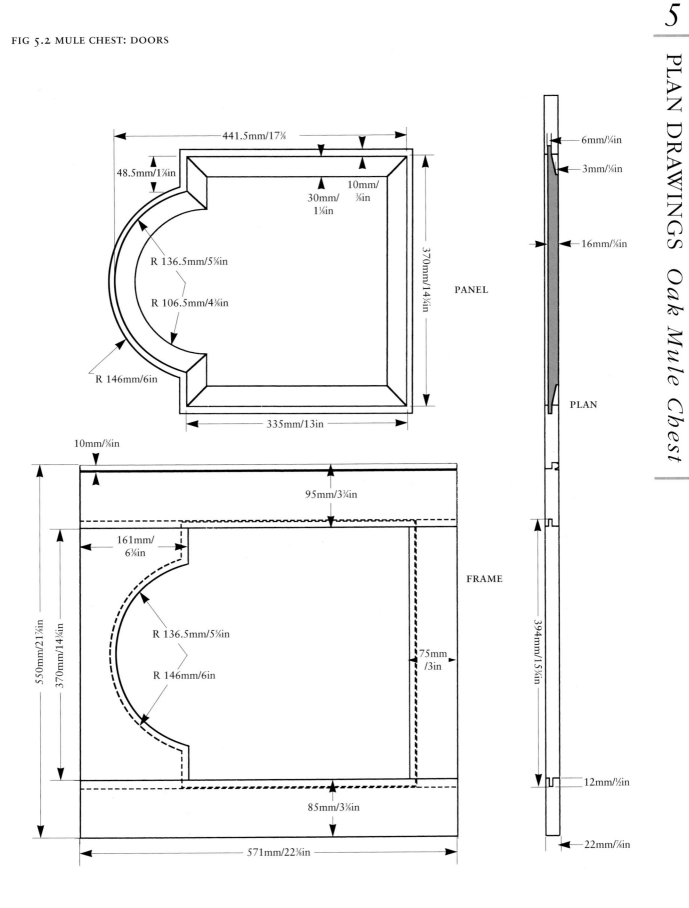

PANEL

FRAME

PLAN

FIG 5.3 MULE CHEST:
CARCASS

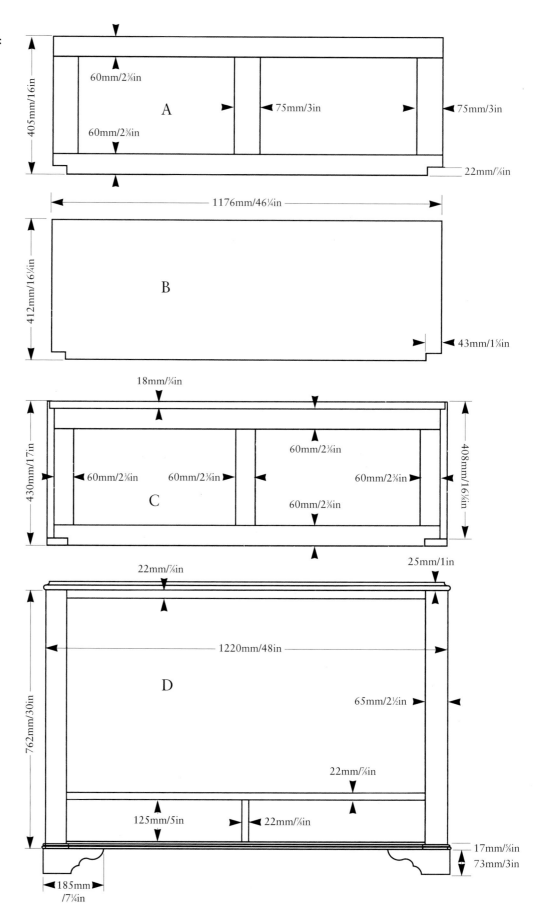

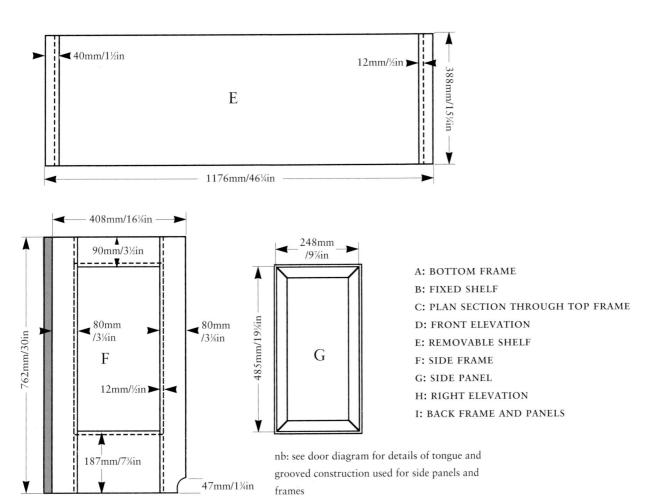

40mm/1½in

12mm/½in

E

388mm/15¼in

1176mm/46¼in

408mm/16⅛in

90mm/3½in

80mm
/3⅛in

80mm
/3⅛in

762mm/30in

F

12mm/½in

187mm/7⅜in

47mm/1¾in

248mm
/9⅞in

485mm/19⅛in

G

A: BOTTOM FRAME

B: FIXED SHELF

C: PLAN SECTION THROUGH TOP FRAME

D: FRONT ELEVATION

E: REMOVABLE SHELF

F: SIDE FRAME

G: SIDE PANEL

H: RIGHT ELEVATION

I: BACK FRAME AND PANELS

nb: see door diagram for details of tongue and grooved construction used for side panels and frames

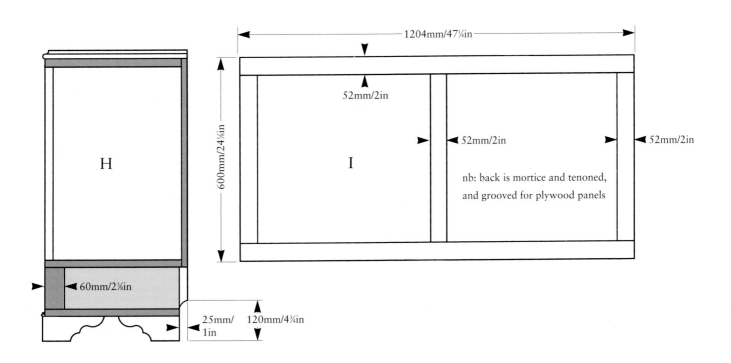

1204mm/47¼in

52mm/2in

52mm/2in

52mm/2in

600mm/24¼in

H

I

nb: back is mortice and tenoned, and grooved for plywood panels

60mm/2⅜in

25mm/
1in

120mm/4¾in

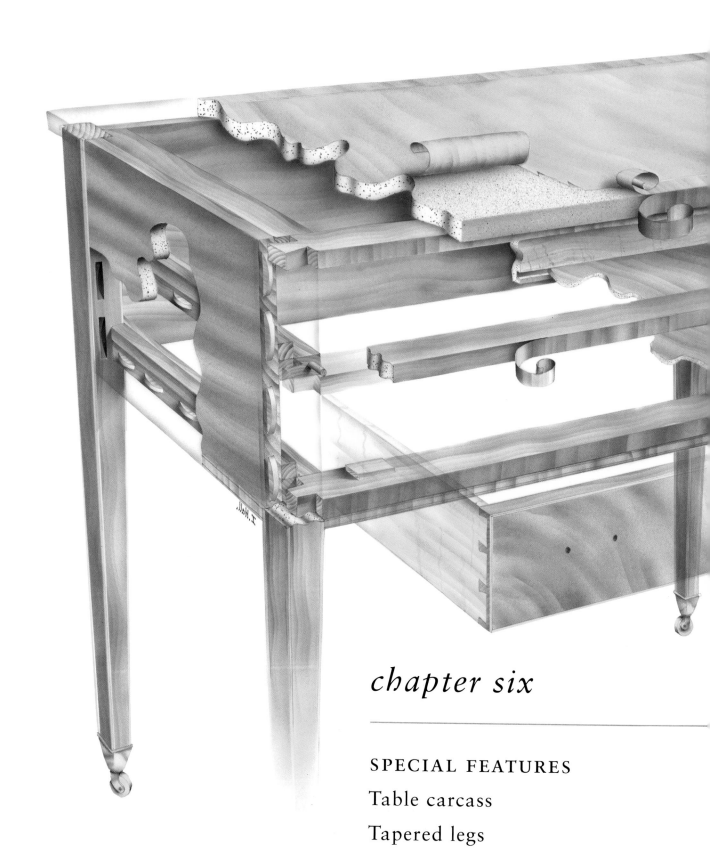

chapter six

SPECIAL FEATURES

Table carcass

Tapered legs

DRESSING TABLE

Even the most elaborate seventeenth- and eighteenth-century furniture relies on relatively simple construction conventions as building blocks. Of these standard forms, none is more adaptable than the table carcass. Basically anything with legs, a flat surface and drawers can be made in this way, including Pembroke and library tables, bonheur-du-jours and Carlton house desks. This little dressing table is a simple example of the form.

The more seventeenth- and eighteenth-century-style furniture I make, the more I am impressed by the versatility of certain standard forms of construction that were developed over that period. Using these relatively simple construction conventions as building blocks, designers and craftsmen satisfied the evermore discerning and demanding markets of the Georgian and Regency periods by producing a great diversity of specialized furniture types without having to reinvent the wheel every time.

This freedom from having to consider the fundamentals of how each piece was to be made must have contributed greatly to the refinement of proportion and decorative treatment that took place over the 100 or so years in question: if it is already known how the piece will be constructed, then more time and imagination can be applied to appearance and detail.

ADAPTING STANDARD FORMS

Of these standard forms, none is more adaptable than the table carcass. It would be possible to spend an entire working life making pieces based on this simple and reliable arrangement without feeling at all restricted. Basically, anything with legs, a flat surface and a drawer or drawers can be made in this way. Pembroke and library tables are obvious, but bonheur-du-jours, Carlton house desks and all manner of complicated-looking furniture can be made by adding a box-carcass superstructure to the top and adjusting a few details.

Further variety can be introduced by truncating the legs so that they are merely corner posts, allowing the carcass to be supported on a pedestal base. Some of the most extravagant Regency furniture was made in this way, sofa tables being a good example, with end standards, pedestal columns on platform bases, scroll-form supports with intermediate platforms, and Regency knee legs all being pressed into service to support the fundamental table carcass.

This dressing table was made several years ago and is almost as simple as a table carcass can be – if it were made with only one drawer it would be the core building block. In appearance it is based on a Sheraton pattern, the original having a split, hinged top which opens to reveal a fitted interior with a mirror rising on an easel. Splendid as this is, the budget didn't allow for so much work, so the proportions were retained but the fitting was restricted to two straightforward drawers.

Boxwood line let into the legs' arrises. Cut tenons for the castors on the legs' ends before assembly

TAPERED LEGS

As, in this construction, all the main carcass parts are jointed into the legs, these should be prepared first. Squareness of these is even more than usually important, as one out-of-square leg will distort the whole carcass, so plane and thickness the stock carefully before forming the taper. The taper starts at the position of the lower drawer rail, and is cut only on the two inner faces of each leg.

Tapered legs may be cut in a number of ways; hand planing is undemanding in the Brazilian mahogany (*Swietania macrophylla*) used here, or simple taper jigs may be made for use with a table saw or thicknesser (see page 144). Of these two options, the thicknesser jig will probably give the better result, unless the grain is particularly interlocked, in which case I recommend the table saw followed by a finely-set hand plane.

STRINGING LINE

If you are working in rosewood (*Dalbergia* spp.), satinwood (*Fagara flava*) or any timber other than mahogany, the next step would be to veneer the legs. If this is the case, pre-cut the veneer, after soaking (see Chapter 4, page 59), to be just smaller than each face of the legs. Remember that the taper is on two faces only, so each face is slightly different. Veneering is straightforward enough; simply veneer each face in turn, though if you are using an especially difficult veneer, it may be better to veneer one pair of opposite faces in one session, leaving the other pair to be completed when the first is dry.

Whether the legs are plain or veneered, a stringing line, for which a rebate just smaller than the line must be cut, is applied to the arrises – boxwood (*Buxus sempervirens*) for dark timbers, black line for others. I cut this rebate with a router inverted in a table. I find that a closed fence – that is, a false fence through which the cutter is plunged, leaving zero clearance – gives the cleanest result. To further ensure a neat rebate, especially on veneered work, back-feed the material in the direction of the cutter's rotation (see page 71). Normally, back-feeding is a bad idea, but in this case the amount of stock removed is so small that, provided a firm grip on the workpiece is maintained, there shouldn't be a problem.

When you have cut rebates in all corners of the legs, glue the line in with PVA, carefully wipe off any surplus, and hold it in place with taut masking tape until dry, before scraping the line flush.

Next, cut a tenon on each leg to fit the square socket castors that you have chosen. Don't leave this till later as it will be much more difficult once the table is assembled.

DRAWER RAILS

The front of the carcass is an archetype of the table carcass in that it is formed by drawer rails, the uppermost being dovetailed into the top of the legs while the others are tenoned into their inner faces. Note that the legs are proud of the carcass rails and sides by the thickness of the stringing line.

I crossbanded the drawer rails to match the drawer fronts; this isn't absolutely necessary as they are mahogany anyway, but it is more in period and unifies the appearance of the piece's front.

Cut the shoulders of the three drawer rails' joints and cut the carcass back to length, all at the same time. Ensure that the dimension between each pair of shoulders is exactly the same, or out-of-square problems will result. Cut mortices in the legs and complete the rails' tenons to fit, then cut the dovetails on the ends of the top rail – the bandsaw is the best tool for this job.

DRAWER RAIL DOVETAIL

This is one of my favourite joints. It looks good, works well and takes little time to make.

First cut the dovetails' shoulders to match those of the lower rails' tenons, then cut the dovetails themselves. All this can be done on the bandsaw with a steady hand and good marking out.

Next, transfer the dovetail shapes to the top of each leg by marking round the tails with a knife, ensuring that the rail is positioned correctly in the fore-and-aft axis of the legs. The sockets can now be roughed out using a router. Clamp each leg in a vice, between two straight offcuts, carefully lining up the top surfaces to give a

Transfer these dovetails to the top of their respective legs by marking round them with a knife, then take out the waste with a router (see panel above) before paring back to the line with a chisel.

Glue up the front legs and drawer rails, tenons first then dovetails.

BISCUITS

In a table carcass, the back and sides are traditionally tenoned or rabbeted into the legs; here I have used biscuits, as the joint is quite long. This allows for a good number of biscuits to be fitted. Less than three No. 20s would be inadequate, but four is plenty in a case such as this where the joints will not be heavily

good running surface for the router. With
care, the router can be guided freehand to
within a whisker of the knife-marked lines

(see above left), after which a quick clean-up with
a chisel results in a perfect fit, as shown in the
photo above.

stressed. Over-sized 'proper' joints can be counter-
productive here, as the amount of wood removed
to make them weakens the leg; biscuits with high-
performance modern adhesives give a good balance.

In original examples I have seen drawer runners
attached in a number of ways:

• glued in place with Scotch glue;
• nailed to the carcass sides (this in an otherwise
  high-quality Pembroke table); and
• dovetailed and tenoned into the legs as with the
  drawer rails.

A larger piece that might be dragged when it is
moved around – a biggish library table for example –

might warrant the extra security provided by dovetails
and tenons, but here the front, sides and back are
screwed to the table's top in any case, and as
previously mentioned, the legs are easily weakened
by the cutting of innumerable mortices and sockets.
Restorers are often faced with the repair of a split leg
as a result of this, so once again, I used biscuits, joining the runners to the carcass sides. To prevent twisting, the runners are cut round the back legs and
pinned into their sides; at the front they are doweled
into the drawer rails.

ASSEMBLY

When gluing up the carcass, the assembly order is
fairly important. The front legs and rails are already

Let in the boxwood line after fitting the drawers to their openings, to avoid narrowing it when adjusting the fit

Oak-veneered MDF is used here for the drawer bottoms, in place of the more traditional solid oak. The bottoms are fitted into slips which are glued to the drawer sides

glued up, so make up the back and back legs, then glue the runners to the sides. When these are dry, complete the carcass by joining the back and front with the sides, checking for square. It is well worth checking the diagonals across the feet as well, as the length of the legs will exaggerate any distortion. To ensure correct spacing, some makers locate the feet in L-shaped blocks (which they set up on the floor or on a gluing-up board) while they glue up the carcass, but I feel that this approach could simply hold the carcass in tension while it is cramped, allowing it to spring back into distortion once the blocks are removed.

APPLIED BANDING

To give the piece a little visual lift, and to relieve the flatness of the carcass, I applied a bought-in satinwood banding to the lower edges of this example. I use the word 'applied' deliberately as it is literally glued onto the surface, not let into a rebate. Not quite proper, I agree, but I rather like the effect.

DRAWERS

The drawers are conventional, being dovetailed with oak (*Quercus* spp.) linings and mahogany fronts.

Veneered MDF bottoms are used here, fitted by means of drawer slips. The fronts are veneered with bookmatched curl mahogany, the central join lining up with that of the table top. Ideally, the grain should run through both drawers and the rails, cut from a single pair of veneers, but this requires very large leaves of veneer, so if you're on a tight budget, it isn't essential. Always veneer drawer fronts after the drawer has been made up: as the front is almost never veneered with a balancer on its back, movement might occur unless it is restrained by the drawer's construction.

Fit a stringing line in the same way as that fitted on the legs, but only after adjusting the fit of the drawers in the carcass, to avoid narrowing the line when you trim their fronts.

TABLE TOP

The top of this piece is veneered onto a groundwork of MDF, which material is highly suitable for Scotch glue veneering, if sanded a little first to scuff the waxy, polished surface as supplied. The following is a description of the order in which this table's top is veneered when using Scotch glue and a hammer – if you are using a vacuum press or similar, the top's

The top is MDF, veneered with
mahogany and crossbanded
with satinwood. A boxwood
line gives definition

veneers and crossbanding must be prepared dry,
taped up and applied as a whole.

The top itself is first cut to finished size, then veneered
on the reverse with plain mahogany. This balancing
veneer is to prevent the cupping that would otherwise
occur if the table top was veneered on its upper
surface only.

Prepare the two leaves of curl mahogany veneer for
the top by sponging them lightly with very hot water,
then pressing them between two boards of MDF or
chipboard for a few hours. Cut sufficient satinwood
crossbanding for the job – a paper-cutting guillotine
is good for this, but a Stanley knife and straightedge
will do. Again, wet the veneer with hot water, then
press it in a stack between the jaws of a vice until
ready to use.

Trim the curl veneers to about 12mm (½in) shorter
than the depth of the top, that is, the measurement
from front to back.

Turn the table top face up, placing newspaper
beneath, and mark a centre line onto the MDF with a
ballpoint pen. Lay the first veneer, with Scotch glue
and a hammer, overlapping this line, then lay the

second overlapping the centre line by the same
amount, but on the other side (see Fig 4.12, page 61).

Lay a wooden straightedge along your marked line
and cut through both veneers with a sharp knife. Peel
off the waste and hammer down the join.

CROSSBANDING

Now, the next step is to trim the laid veneers to take
the crossbanding. I generally use a sharp cutting
gauge for this, running along the edge of the
groundwork, but again, a wooden straightedge and
knife will do. Whichever you use, cut a perimeter
that is slightly smaller in depth than the combined
width of your crossbanding and boxwood line, then
peel off the waste.

If any gelled glue or chips of veneer remain on this
perimeter, run an old chisel along it to clean it off.

Lay the crossbanding and line at the same time,
working quickly and hammering towards the main
veneer. Cut each join by the overlap technique, and
when you reach a corner do the same, cutting the
mitre through both layers. When it has dried, the
crossbanding should overhang the edge by a fraction,

A simplified version of a
Sheraton design for a dressing
table, in mahogany and
satinwood with boxwood line

and should be trimmed off square and flush. A
block plane, angled downwards, will perform this
task neatly, but on a large table you will save time
by running a router, fitted with a flush-trimming,
bearing-guided cutter, along the edges before
reaching for the block plane.

Crossband the edge of the table top in the same way
and clean it off carefully using the block plane,
followed by abrasive. Be very careful not to damage
the veneer when trimming like this and resist the
temptation to use a plane, however sharp and finely
set, on the face of veneer, as this will tear it off the
groundwork. Instead, use a cabinet scraper to level
anything too delicate for the belt sander, then make
judicious use of abrasives, either by hand, with a
random orbital sander, or with a palm sander.

To finish, I bodied-up the table with an amber
varnish and gave it a slightly 'dirty' French polish
so that it didn't look too new, before fitting the
castors and handles.

This table was quick to make, and I hope that some
of the possibilities for building on it are apparent –
slightly heavier legs and a glazed superstructure on
top as a display cabinet perhaps?

FIG 6.1 DRESSING TABLE: CONSTRUCTION

6

PLAN DRAWINGS Dressing Table

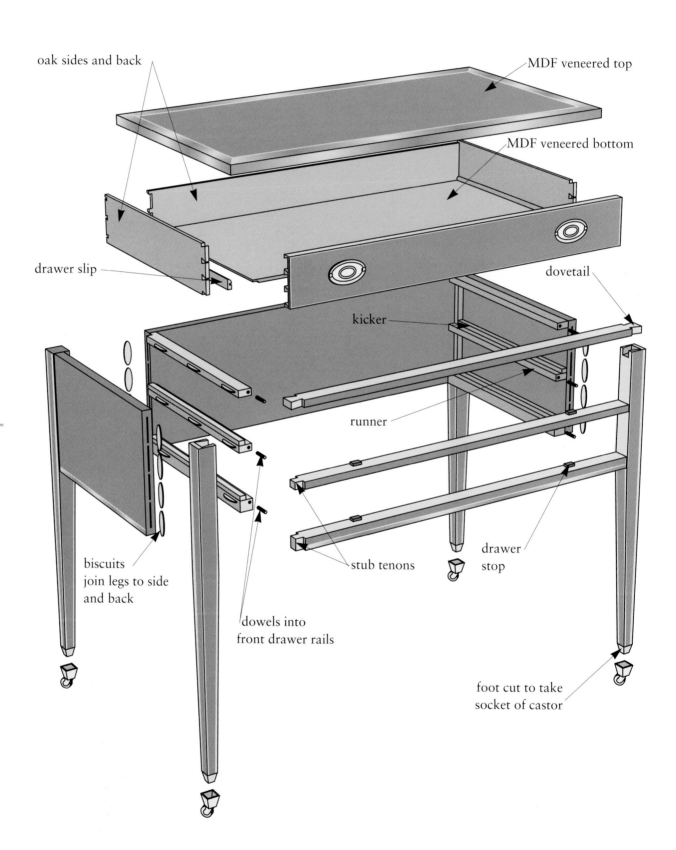

oak sides and back

MDF veneered top

MDF veneered bottom

drawer slip

dovetail

kicker

runner

biscuits
join legs to side
and back

stub tenons

drawer
stop

dowels into
front drawer rails

foot cut to take
socket of castor

6

PLAN DRAWINGS *Dressing Table*

FIG 6.2 DRESSING TABLE: PLAN VIEWS

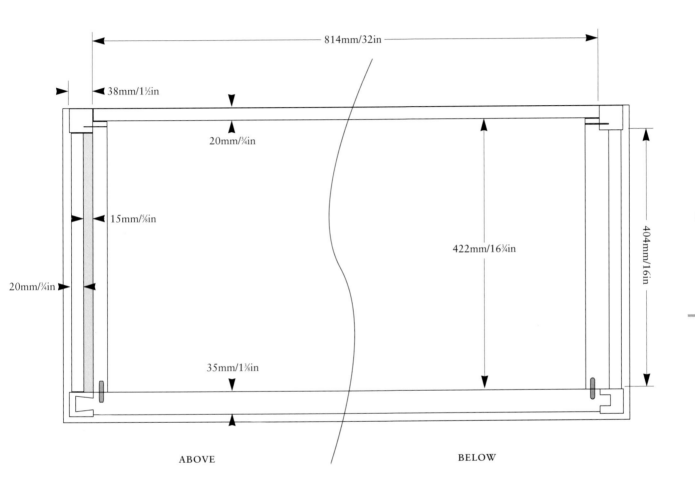

814mm/32in

38mm/1½in

20mm/¾in

15mm/⅝in

20mm/¾in

422mm/16¾in

404mm/16in

35mm/1⅜in

ABOVE

BELOW

113

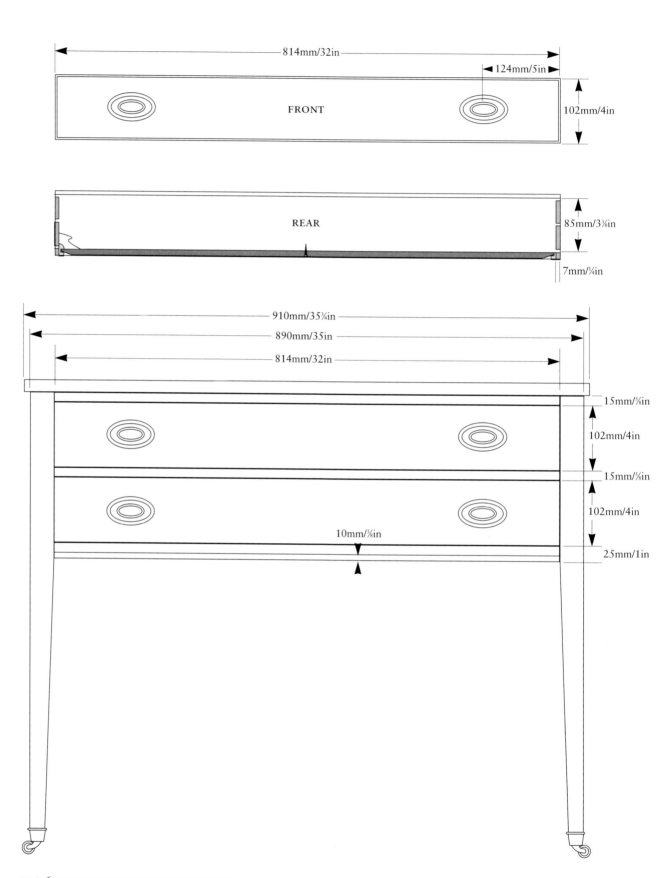

814mm/32in

124mm/5in

FRONT

102mm/4in

REAR

85mm/3⅜in

7mm/¼in

910mm/35⅞in

890mm/35in

814mm/32in

15mm/⅝in

102mm/4in

15mm/⅝in

102mm/4in

10mm/⅜in

25mm/1in

FIG 6.3 DRESSING TABLE: ELEVATIONS

FIG 6.4 DRESSING TABLE: DRAWER

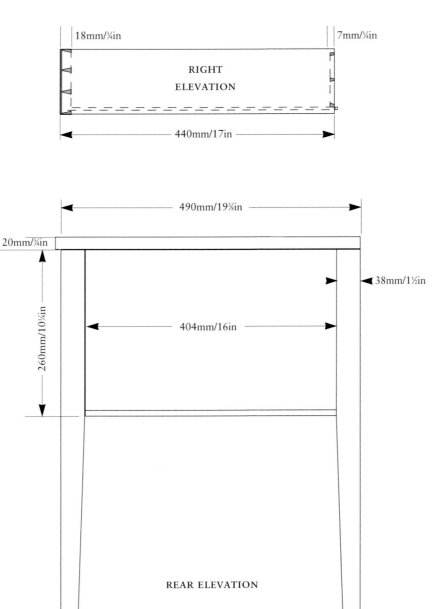

18mm/¾in

7mm/¼in

RIGHT
ELEVATION

440mm/17in

490mm/19⅜in

20mm/¾in

38mm/1½in

260mm/10¼in

404mm/16in

720mm/28¼in

REAR ELEVATION

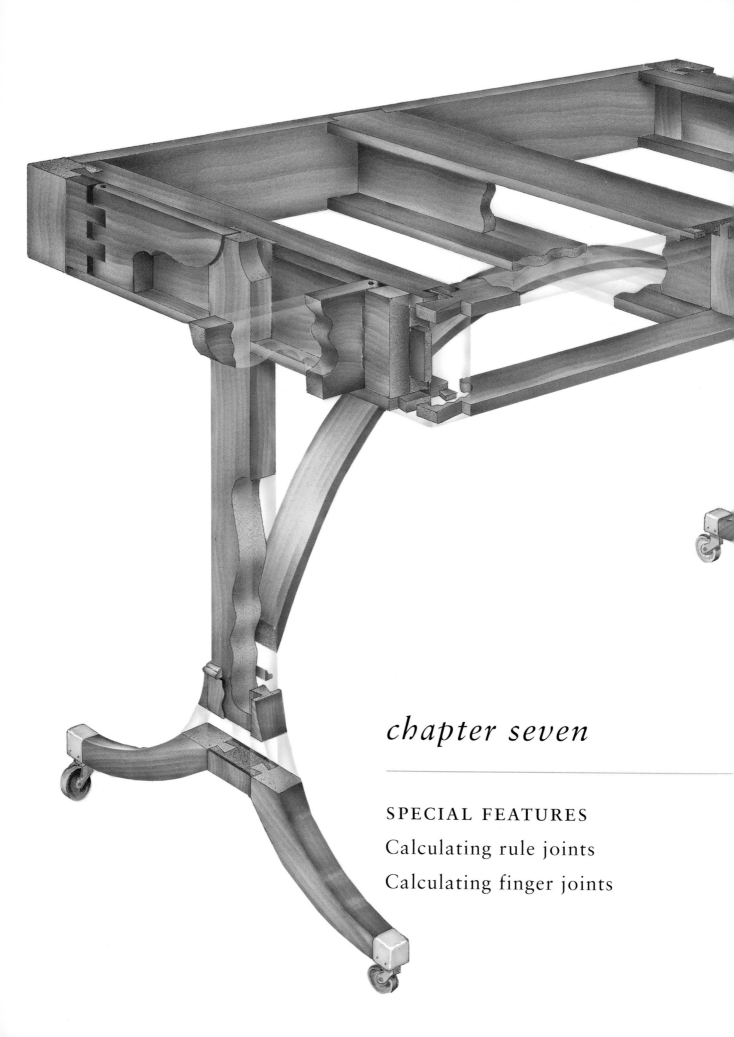

chapter seven

SPECIAL FEATURES
Calculating rule joints
Calculating finger joints

SOFA TABLE

Refinements of furniture forms and functions reached a pinnacle in the late eighteenth and early nineteenth centuries, tables in particular being made for specific purposes. As its name suggests, the sofa table was developed to stand behind the newly introduced sofa, which purpose dictates its long, narrow proportions. Favourites among the designers of the period for their decorative possibilities, sofa tables exploit almost all cabinetmaking skills.

Thought of as a Regency furniture type, the sofa table actually appeared towards the end of the eighteenth century, gradually superseding the Pembroke table, from which it was developed. Sofa tables are named for their intended purpose, to stand against a sofa, which also dictates their elegant proportions – longer and thinner than the squarish Pembroke and usually fitted with two drawers rather than one.

A more significant departure from the Pembroke is in the treatment of the sofa table's legs. A Pembroke usually stands on fine, tapered legs, either square or turned. These suit the delicacy of the form, but would look plain and spindly on the longer and more substantial sofa table. Instead, end standards, or sometimes single pedestals, support the carcass. This provides an opportunity for some very stylish work. Variations include the relatively restrained column-and-leg arrangement used here, more exuberant lyre-shaped standards, bizarre concoctions of turned and carved elements and platform-leg-and-column forms (see the extending table in Chapter 8). Even the stretcher offers scope for experiment, from turning and carving to veneering.

Because of this, the sofa table comes as close to being a 'sampler' of cabinetmaking techniques as any piece

Sofa table in Brazilian
rosewood veneer,
with laminated arc stretcher

I have come across. Carcass-making, drawer-
dovetailing, veneering, rule and finger joints – use a
turned stretcher and, with shaped legs, pretty much
everything is covered in one project.

VENEERS AND VENEERING

The veneer used for this example, one of a pair, is from
my dwindling stock of Brazilian rosewood (*Dalbergia
nigra*) which, together with mahogany (*Swietenia* spp.),
satinwood (*Fagara flava*) and maccassar ebony
(*Diasporus ebenum*), is contemporary with the design.
These are less than environmentally friendly even as
veneers, so figured sycamore (*Acer pseudoplatanus*)
could be used instead, and a crown-cut walnut (*Juglans*
spp.) makes a convincing faded mahogany if bleached.
Stain sycamore grey and it becomes 'harewood' in
Georgian parlance; likewise, rosewood is 'palisander'
and maccassar ebony 'coromandel'.

I used Scotch glue and a hammer for all the veneering
in this table. Any other method may be used, of course,
but I do recommend hot glue as it is not only in period
but is also suitable for both flat and curved work.
Remember to sponge the veneer with near-boiling water
an hour or two before use, laying it between two flat
boards to render it workable (see Chapter 4, page 59).

TABLE TOP

The top of this table is constructed from 15mm (⅝in) MDF, veneered on both sides. The edges are also veneered, but where the rule joints are formed, a solid mahogany lipping is used. First, prepare the groundwork. Cut the MDF to size and apply the lipping (see Fig 7.1 and panel, page 122) with size '0' biscuits or a cross-grained loose tongue. Make templates for the radius of the table top's corners and the inner radius of the crossbanding from offcuts.

Apply a balancing veneer to the underside of the table top, with the grain direction across the width, and lay the pieces veneer-side down on newspaper to prevent bowing. Veneer the main body of the face side, again with the grain running across the width, allowing an overlap on to the area to be crossbanded but finishing short of the MDF's edge.

Trim these edges with a cutting gauge set to the intended width of the crossbanding and cut the radiused corners with a sharp knife, using the smaller radius template. The crossbanding can now be applied. A stringing line will be routed in after the rule joints are done.

Rule joints cause much consternation. This might have been justified when they were worked entirely by hand, but with matched cove and round-over cutters for the router they present no problems. The key to success with these joints is to pay careful attention to the pivot point of the hinge (see panel, page 122). Draw a cross section of the joint using the dimensions of your cutters and hinges, and make sure that the centre of the hinge's pin is accurately transferred to the drawing. This marks the centre of the radius to be cut with the round-over cutter, and gives the depth of the quirk at the top of the radius. Using this as a guide to depth of cut, rout the round-over. Now the cove can be routed to match; increase the depth of cut by increments until the two sides of the joint fit perfectly with a piece of paper between them as clearance.

To complete the joint a small clearance radius, again centred on the hinge pin's pivot point, must be cut on the underside of the round-over to allow the hinge action. Once this has been done, the hinges can be fitted. Note that their knuckles sit inside the round-over, so cut their recesses carefully to avoid any breaking through.

THE RULE JOINT

A successful rule joint depends on two things:

1 *matching the radius of the two parts; and*
2 *fixing the pivot point at their centre.*

With a matched pair of router cutters, cove (core box) and round-over, the first of these is easy. The second is fixed by the centre of the hinge pin. As the unequal-leaf table hinge is fitted with the knuckle inwards and the face flush, the equation for finding the pivot point from the table's top is:

pivot point = table top thickness – distance from centre of hinge pin to outer face of hinge

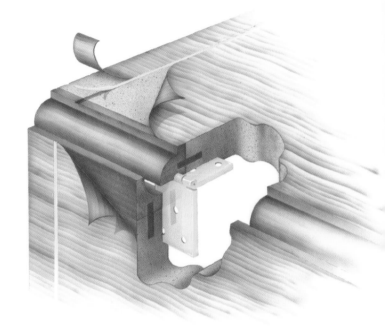

Cutaway view of rule joint

With the hinges fitted, trim the edges of the top to finished size, and radius the corners using the larger radius template. Now, using a router, cut a groove to take a boxwood (*Buxus sempervirens*) line between the main veneer and crossbanding. This should be left slightly proud, to be scraped and sanded flush when dry. All that remains to complete the top is to crossband the edges and sand to a finish.

THE CARCASS

Construction

This type of carcass (see Fig 7.5), with minor variations, may be used for all those tables with drawers of which the Georgians were so fond.

All parts are mahogany except where they might be worn by the drawers, in which case they are oak (*Quercus robur*). Thus, back, sides, divider and corner blocks are mahogany; drawer rails, muntin and runners are oak. The Georgians would perhaps have used Baltic pine where I have used mahogany.

Back and sides are jointed to the corner blocks with single-shouldered tenons – biscuits could be used instead, although the length of the joint allows room for only two. The front assembly comprises two drawer rails, which are dovetailed into the top and bottom of the front corner blocks, and a drawer-dividing muntin, which is jointed to the top and bottom drawer rails with double tenons.

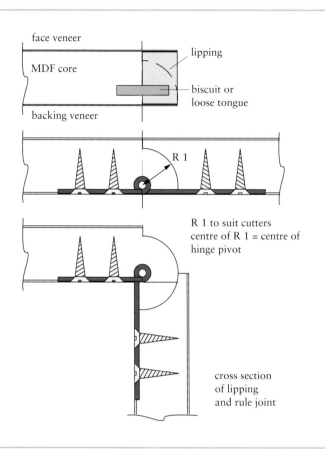

face veneer

MDF core

lipping

biscuit or
loose tongue

backing veneer

R 1

R 1 to suit cutters
centre of R 1 = centre of
hinge pivot

cross section
of lipping
and rule joint

Typically, the table top thickness might be 18mm (¾in) and the distance from the centre of the hinge pin 3mm (⅛in), in which case the pivot point would be 15mm (⅝in) from the top surface. So, with a set of 12mm (½in) cove and round-over router cutters, the quirk at the top of the joint will be 3mm (⅛in): 15–12mm (⅝–½in). Round over the lipping to this setting first, then cut the cove, making shallow passes until the joint fits; a piece of paper between the two parts will give the tolerance necessary for smooth operation.

Unless you are using biscuits, cut mortices for single-shouldered tenons into the rear corner blocks, then work the tenons for the back and sides to fit. The back can be glued to its corner blocks at this point.

It is best to cut the shoulders for the dovetails on the front rails from a stop on the radial arm saw, then cut the dovetails themselves using a simple jig on the bandsaw. On such a small construction, any inaccuracy will send the job out of square, so all parts must be exactly matching in their dimension between shoulders.

The sockets are marked from the tails with a knife, and cut to depth. The drawer muntin is fitted next, not forgetting to work a 6mm (¼in) groove in its back edge before assembly, using a double mortice and tenon. The front rails, muntin and corner blocks can then be glued up.

Glue the sides and divider to the front and back, then fit the drawer runners, again marking the sockets from the dovetails; where these form a joint with the drawer rails, they should be half lapped. When all is dry, the outside of the now-complete carcass should be cleaned up, making sure all joints are flush, and its veneer prepared as previously described.

VENEERING

Cut the crossbanding for the drawer rails as accurately as possible – no more than 1.5mm (¹⁄₁₆in) oversize –

The use of rosewood for both the main veneer and crossbanding is a restrained treatment, given definition by boxwood stringing. Period examples are often quite showy, with coromandel (macassar ebony) veneer and brass inlay, rosewood with satinwood crossbanding, or even more striking combinations

to make cleaning up easier, and prepare eight rectangles for the corner blocks. Two bookmatched pieces for the false drawer fronts and crossbanding for the false rails will also be needed.

With these pieces to hand, veneer the carcass, starting with the front. Glue will go everywhere when crossbanding the drawer rails and you must clean this up as you go: if you leave it to dry it will take hours to remove neatly.

It is most important to work quickly while veneering the carcass – I normally allow 30 minutes for this, including cleaning up.

When the carcass veneer is dry and trimmed, inlay a stringing line around the false drawer fronts, using the router as before, then sand carefully to a finish and set aside until assembly.

DRAWERS

The hand-dovetailed drawers are entirely traditional, with mahogany fronts, oak linings and oak bottoms.

Veneer the fronts after the drawer has been assembled but before the bottom is fitted (see Fig 7.3). Fit the drawers to the carcass and make any necessary adjustments before proceeding to the next stage, applying a stringing line, thus avoiding any reduction in its width.

Rout a rebate just smaller than the stringing around the front edges of the drawer fronts and then, using PVA and taut masking tape, glue it in place. It is best to work round each drawer front, mitring as you go. Finish with a long side as this will allow some flexibility in the fit of the last mitre.

FINGER JOINTS

If anything, finger joints are an exercise in careful marking out, the object being to achieve a large wooden hinge. As with rule joints, the pivot point is the crucial factor (see panel on page 126). Traditionally, finger joints were made from beech (*Fagus sylvatica*), but this is the woodworm's diet of choice, as any restorer will tell you, so for these pieces I used mahogany.

THE FINGER JOINT

First cut the two parts to the castellated shapes shown – the width of the fingers is the overall width of the stock divided by five, so for an overall width of 100mm (4in), each finger will be 20mm (⅘in) wide.

Now the back of each finger must be rounded over to radius 1 (see below), a radius of half the stock's width; for 20mm (⅘in) stock this radius will be 10mm (⅖in).

X

Y

Y = X/5

CASTELLATED SHAPE OF
FLAP SUPPORT

scalloped relief
to reverse forms
finger pull

joint
closed

joint half open

OPERATION OF
FINGER JOINT

joint fully open

R 1

Ø 5mm

pivot hole shown
as 5mm should
be drilled to suit
available pin

20mm

R 2

20mm

PLAN VIEW OF
FINGER JOINT

When making batches of these joints, it is useful to have a sliding box jig on the table saw, but as only four are needed for this project it is probably as quick, and is certainly more satisfying, to cut them by hand. When doing so, treat them as dovetails; cut one side using a back saw or bandsaw for the rip cuts, follow this with the coping saw and chisel to complete the sockets, then mark the second side from the first. When all four have been completed, screw-fix them to the carcass from the inside.

END STANDARDS

The style of end standard used for this piece is simple in form (see Fig 7.4), but post-Georgian experience tells us that this area is the weak point of the sofa table – many repairs to the legs of period examples have been required, most as a result of joint or short-grain failure following too great a weight being placed on the table. Select the uprights from straight-grained mahogany but cut the legs from stock with a grain that follows the curve of the leg as closely as possible, as including any short grain is asking for trouble.

Prepare a ply or MDF template for the legs, remembering to allow for the sliding dovetail. It is best to cut this joint line straight and square first, and even to work the dovetail, before bandsawing the legs to shape, as a large bearing surface is helpful.

My usual approach to the leg-to-upright joint is to set up a dovetail cutter in an inverted router, first

To allow the joint to open, the back of each socket must be scooped out to radius 2 (see below left) to give clearance for the front edge of the fingers; for 20mm (⅞in) stock, this radius will be 14mm (⁹⁄₁₆in). Plenty of clearance can be allowed as this part is not seen.

Finally, the hole for the pivot pin must be drilled (see below left). This must be exactly centred on the stock, and half the stock's thickness from the ends of the fingers. For this example the distance is 10mm (⅜in). Drill the hole with the joint assembled and correctly lined up to ensure smooth operation – drilling halfway through from each end will minimize any run-out. Match the drill's diameter to the available pin – a 5in (125mm) round wire nail will work well.

Detail of flap supports

cutting the female part in the upright. Without adjusting the height of the cutter, the male part may be cut on the legs to a high degree of accuracy by judicious adjustment of the router table's fence. Take a little off each side, one side at a time, and check the fit in the mating part.

After bandsawing, I finish the profile of the legs with an inverted router fitted with a bearing-guided, flush-trimming cutter that runs against the template pinned to the work. This involves some cutting against the grain and is a little nerve-wracking. If you prefer, the legs can instead be finished using either drum and disc sanders or even a spokeshave and rasp. Whichever you choose, the surface finish is not critical as it will later be veneered.

The uprights must be veneered and bound on their edges with stringing before the standards can be assembled. Veneer their faces first, then trim the veneer at the edges while it and the glue are moist. The edges can then be crossbanded without waiting for the faces to dry.

The boxwood stringing is fitted into a rebate which should be cut into the corners of the standards with a bearing-guided router cutter in the same way as for the drawer fronts. Glue the stringing with PVA, carefully wipe off any surplus, and hold it in place with taut masking tape. Sand the standards, then glue up the sliding dovetails and fit the plates which 'block out' the base of the upright. Veneer and bind the legs in the same way as the uprights, then apply a moulding around the top of the leg blocks. After cleaning up, cut tenons on the legs to fit the castors.

A sofa table with arc stretcher,
in the late Georgian style

LAMINATING THE STRETCHERS

The arc stretchers in this piece (see Fig 7.2) are laminated in mahogany but any straight-grained timber will do as the whole is subsequently veneered. Make the radius around a former of a slightly tighter curve than that required, as the finished laminate will spring back slightly when the clamps are removed. Five laminates is about right for this radius. Veneer the faces and crossband the edges, then make scarf cuts at each end for fitting to the standards on assembly.

As an alternative, a turned stretcher is entirely appropriate for this piece. If you choose this option, the turning should be spigoted into the centre of the blocking-out plates at the base of the end standards. The sofa table as a form has been widely used, and most books on antique furniture will provide ideas for variations of both standards and stretchers.

ASSEMBLY AND POLISHING

Finally, the carcass sides must be prepared for the standards by relieving the outer sides of the drawer runners – this should be marked from the standards themselves. To give further stability to this joint, create a shoulder on the inner face of each standard by dressing away (see Fig 7.4). This will provide a mechanical location for the carcass-to-standard joint, and relieve the load on the screws. French polishing should be carried out before the now completed sub-assemblies are put together. The precise polishing process will vary according to the veneer chosen, and indeed the preferred finishing material, but if a stain or any but the palest of pale polishes is used, the boxwood lines must first be masked with a carefully applied line of clear polish, then scraped clean before the final rubbers.

For this table my client asked that it not look too new, so rather than distress it, a 'dirty' polish was deliberately introduced. This polish builds up in internal corners as it is applied, to produce an effect that mimics years of dirt.

To assemble the table, lay the top face down on a soft blanket and fix the carcass to it with screws through the top drawer rails and runners. I have occasionally seen the evidence of an over-long or too zealously countersunk screw causing a pimple in a table top, so exercise caution.

Fix the standards to the carcass with screws from the inside, then screw and plug the stretcher to the inner sides of the standards and the bottom of the central drawer runner.

FIG 7.1
TABLE TOP: PLAN VIEW
SHOWING VENEER LAYOUT

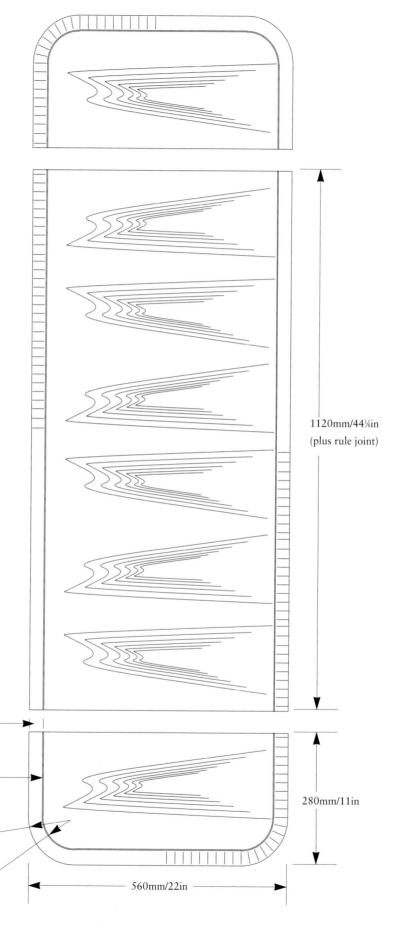

1120mm/44⅛in
(plus rule joint)

30mm/1⁷⁄₁₆in

2mm/¹⁄₁₆in

R 100mm/4in

R 68mm/2½in

280mm/11in

560mm/22in

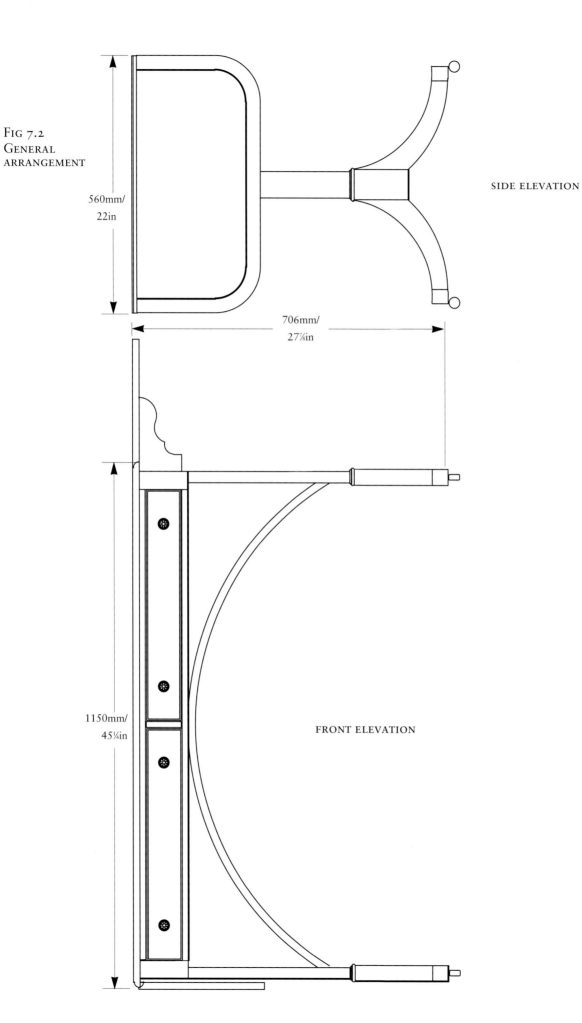

Fig 7.2
General
arrangement

560mm/
22in

SIDE ELEVATION

706mm/
27⅞in

1150mm/
45¼in

FRONT ELEVATION

FIG 7.3
DRAWER:
CONSTRUCTION

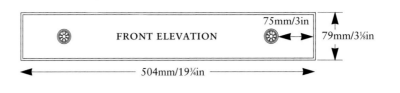

FRONT ELEVATION

75mm/3in

79mm/3⅛in

504mm/19¾in

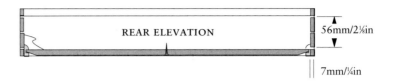

REAR ELEVATION

56mm/2⅛in

7mm/¼in

500mm/19⅝in

RIGHT ELEVATION

18mm/¾in

7mm/¼in

FIG 7.4
END STANDARDS:
CONSTRUCTION

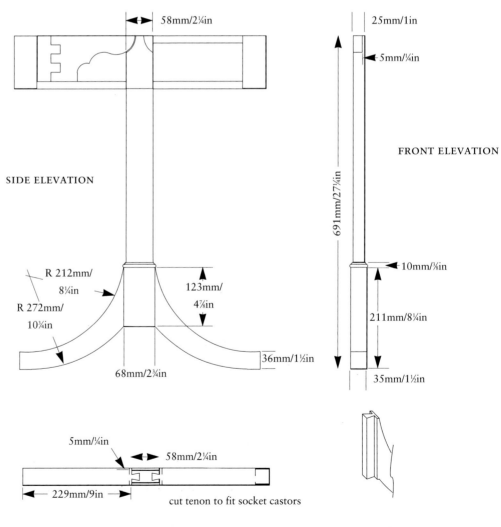

58mm/2¼in

25mm/1in

5mm/¼in

SIDE ELEVATION

FRONT ELEVATION

691mm/27¼in

R 212mm/
8¼in

123mm/
4⅞in

10mm/⅜in

R 272mm/
10¾in

211mm/8¼in

36mm/1½in

68mm/2¾in

35mm/1½in

5mm/¼in

58mm/2¼in

229mm/9in

cut tenon to fit socket castors

UNDERSIDE PLAN VIEW

LEG JOINT DETAIL

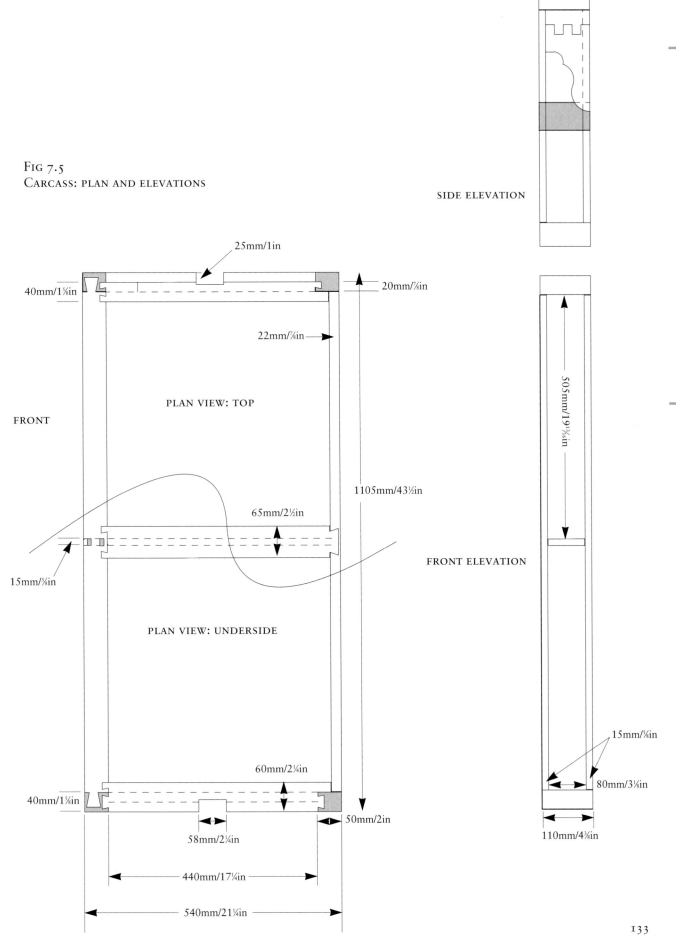

Fig 7.5
CARCASS: PLAN AND ELEVATIONS

SIDE ELEVATION

25mm/1in

40mm/1⅝in

20mm/⅞in

22mm/⅞in

PLAN VIEW: TOP

FRONT

1105mm/43½in

65mm/2½in

505mm/19¾in

15mm/⅝in

FRONT ELEVATION

PLAN VIEW: UNDERSIDE

15mm/⅝in

80mm/3⅛in

60mm/2¼in

40mm/1⅝in

50mm/2in

58mm/2¼in

110mm/4⅜in

440mm/17¼in

540mm/21¼in

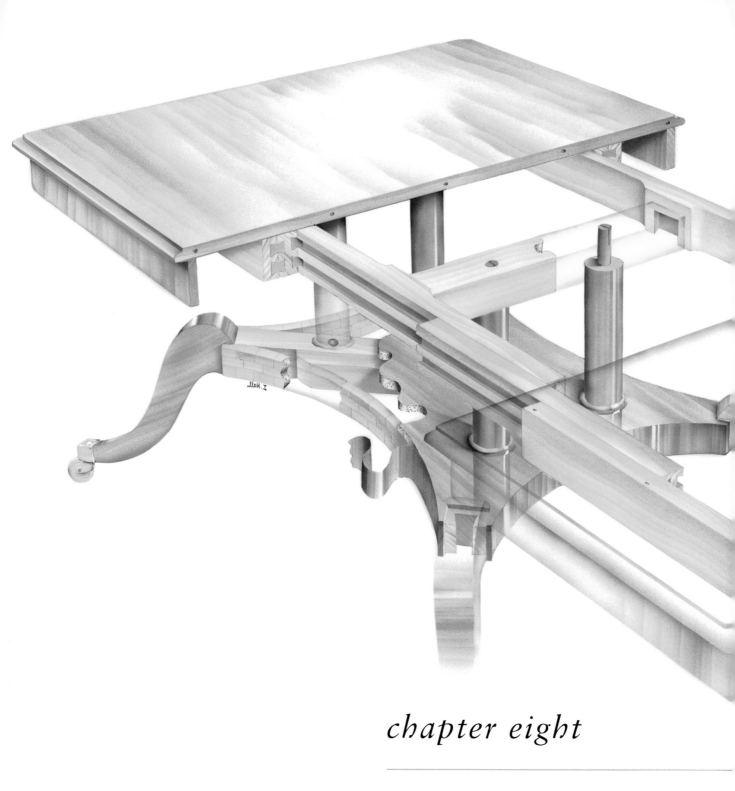

chapter eight

SPECIAL FEATURES
Telescopic runners
Platform stretcher

EXTENDING TABLE

Both pedestal and extending tables became popular in the eighteenth century, but few examples were made which combine both features, due to the inherent difficulties in reconciling a central support with the mechanics of variable size. This table, in a late Georgian style, overcomes the problem by using a telescopic runner pack supported on a substantial leg and platform stretcher arrangement.

The phrase 'necessity is the mother of invention' is never truer than when designing and making furniture. I will go further and say that it is most difficult to come up with an idea when there are no constraints of necessity to be worked within – an entirely open brief is the hardest to fulfil.

Having said this, sometimes a client can ask for a piece which, on first consideration, can't be made at all due to apparent contradictions between its form and function. The ensuing process of research and problem-solving can be frustrating, but can also teach us a lot about furniture design and construction – more, certainly, than simply knocking out another version of a piece that we already know how to make.

MEETING THE BRIEF

This extending table is a good illustration in point. The brief was for a piece to be used primarily as a centre table for reading, writing and the comfortable accommodation of four diners, but for occasional use as an eight- to ten-seater dining table. This is a reasonable requirement and in itself presents no unusual problems, until the specified appearance is considered: when in its more commonly used four-seater form, it is not to look like a dining table at all, having a pedestal base.

Pedestal centre tables were popular throughout the late-Georgian, Regency and Victorian periods. They were most often circular and supported by a single column, which usually sat on a tripartite platform with feet and castors. They are an attractive class of table and lend themselves well to the snap-top approach, in which the table top is hinged to the vertical in order that it might be placed against a wall when not in use, but do not offer much scope for extending.

During the Victorian period, some extending pedestal tables were made with great heavy bases that split, enabling them to be drawn apart and thus providing the necessary support to the ends of the top as leaves were inserted. The inherent heaviness of this approach ruled it out for this table, however. Other tables were built on the draw-leaf principle, allowing for the insertion of a single, small leaf, but this would not provide anywhere near enough room for ten place settings.

This doesn't mean that history provides no solution, just that period elements have to be combined in a

The table in extended form, with two leaves inserted. Considerable leverage forces act on the base and runners in this arrangement, so large sections and strong joints must be used. When photographed, the table had been in use for several years without problems

new way. The first step is to provide support as close to the four corners of the unextended top as possible. This can be achieved by exploiting the style of platform base used quite widely on sofa, side and centre tables by late-Georgian and Regency makers. In this style of base, good-sized legs start almost below the top's corners and arch upwards and inwards to be fixed on a platform near the vertical mid-point of the base, while the table itself sits on scrolled supports or turned columns fixed to the platform. This arrangement results in a centre table which is as stable as if it had a straightforward leg at each corner and, if built strongly, will bear the leverage imposed by an extended top.

Now that the decision has been made not to extend the base, all that is required is a means of extending the top. My solution was to use a runner pack based on the sliding-dovetail-slip principle, in which two five-section telescopic runners are made, with the centre runners fixed to the base, the outer runners fixed to the main table top, and the intervening runners floating.

A word of advice – do not attempt an extending table of any complexity without making full-size detail drawings in plan and in both elevations. Moving parts introduce a wide range of variables which must be thoroughly considered before committing tool to timber.

RUNNER PACK

Starting with the runner pack is usual, as all else is straightforward and must accommodate the moving parts.

Timber

Whenever I have a piece to make which requires optimum strength and stability, I use well-dried rock maple (*Acer saccharum*). This timber is close grained, available in large sizes and sections free of knots and other faults, and it machines cleanly, if with some difficulty. Maple's wear characteristics are such that it has been used extensively for dance floors, and its stability has made it a standard timber for musical instrument makers – all in all, a highly suitable choice for extending runners.

The runner pack is made entirely from this hard-wearing stuff, in sections deep enough to withstand deflection under the heavy load imposed by the leverage of the extended table top – don't forget that the table will be loaded and a diner may well lean

The telescopic runner
pack is made from large
sections of maple, a timber
with good wear and stability
characteristics as well
as strength

upon it, so it must be able to withstand considerably more than its own weight.

Construction

Variations of the dovetail-slip runner may be found in furniture made over a wide period; sometimes the dovetail is replaced by a T-section, but this results in a sloppier fit.

The principle used here is simple – dovetail-section slips run in dovetail slots machined in the runners' sides, thus allowing a telescopic action while maintaining close contact of the sliding faces. Each slip is fixed to one runner side, thus acting as a stop. On a smaller table, one slip per side is adequate, but here two are used, in consideration of the high loading. This more than doubles the assembly's capacity in terms of shear and torsion stresses.

Once the drawing is made, preparing the runner pack is straightforward enough, and best done on a router table. First plane and thickness the stock for the runners, paying particular attention to its squareness. Cross-cut the maple generously over-length, as the first and last couple of inches of each runner won't machine accurately and must be considered sacrificial, to be trimmed after routing.

The next task is to rout dovetail slots in the meeting faces of the runners. Maple is a hard timber and not the easiest material to machine, so it is prudent to remove waste from the slots with a table saw or similar before proceeding to the routing stage.

Rout the dovetail slots using a suitable dovetail cutter and a router table, being careful to cut both slots from the same datum edge to ensure parallel. First choose the edges to serve as datum – the top edge makes most sense – then mark it clearly to avoid confusion while machining. Next set up a router, fitted with a suitable dovetail cutter, in a router table and set the table's fence for the first set of slots. Machine these, being careful to maintain even pressure both against the fence and down onto the table, then re-position the fence for the second set of slots.

Leave the router and cutter set up, as the slips must be machined with the cutter at exactly the same height as the slots. Prepare more maple than will be needed to the outer dimensions of the slips (the length will be twice the height of the cut just made and the width, the diameter of the cutter at its widest point), then position the router table's fence to machine one side of the slips. Complete one side of all pieces in this way, then machine the other side of

Here the dovetail slip arrangement can be seen. The use of double slips and slots improves tracking and increases load-bearing ability, but requires accurate machining to achieve smooth running

As the runner frame is seen whenever the table is opened or closed, the top edges are moulded for a neater appearance. Note that the centre runner, which is dovetailed to the cross-members, is dressed away to reduce bulk while retaining good jointing area, and the column spigots are wedged

a test piece. Test this for fit in the slots, then adjust the table's fence as necessary.

Spend some time adjusting the set-up to make the slips exactly right: they can be adjusted afterwards, but it's easier to make them accurately at the machining stage. Wax the slips, slots and meeting faces of the runners after assembly to reduce friction.

Assembly

The two fixed, centre runners are linked by two cross-pieces, forming a frame which is the main structural component of the table. Wedged tenons could be used for these joints, but it is better to let gravity help rather than hinder, so I decided to use substantial dovetails. To allow enough material for the female part of this joint, without unnecessary visual bulk, the centre runners are dressed away on their inner faces (see photo, right).

The centre section can now be glued up, after running an ovolo moulding on the upper edges to tidy it up: this part will, unlike most table underframes, be seen every time the table is extended or retracted.

Before assembling the runner pack, plane a little from the top edge of each intermediate runner – 1mm

(½in) is enough – to stop it binding on the underside of the table top. The process of assembly must be carried out in the correct order. First, fix one pair of slips to the inner face and end of an intermediate runner. Next, slide this onto a centre runner, and overshoot to leave room to fix another pair of slips to the outer face and end of this centre runner. Following that, slide the intermediate runner back over this second pair of slips to leave room to fit the opposite intermediate runner in the same way. With this done, slips can then be fixed to the outer face and edge of the intermediate runner, and the inner face and edge of the outer runner, which are slid together last of all.

COLUMNS

The runner assembly is supported by four substantial, turned mahogany (*Swietania macrophylla*) columns. These are jointed to the runner assembly at the top and the platform at the bottom, by turned spigots fitted into drilled mortices. The spigots are both glued and wedged for security but even so, it is important that the spigots are accurately turned to suit the drill that will be used for their mortices, so drill a test hole in a piece of scrap and use this rather than callipers to check the dimension while turning.

BASE

As previously mentioned, the leverage imposed on the base by the fully-extended top is considerable, and if any weak points are allowed to creep in at the base, especially at the leg-to-platform joint, failure is almost guaranteed.

Consequently, the platform itself is a non-structural, decorative superstructure concealing a substantial maple framework. To make this, halve two pieces of maple together to form an X, then glue and screw leg bearers, maple again, inside the 90° angles formed by the X – but not before routing or band-sawing a dovetail socket into the end of each one to accept the legs' dovetails.

Next, fix a suitably shaped piece of 12mm (½in) MDF to the top of the framework to serve as the platform's top, then build up the curved sides brick-fashion from band-sawn blocks of mahogany. Although laminated sides would do just as well, as the whole platform is finished with a mahogany veneer, these bricks are a good way of using up the small hardwood offcuts which seem to proliferate in most furniture workshops.

With the cover plate removed, the underside of the base reveals the maple structure which provides strength. Leg bearers, to which the legs are dovetailed, are jointed to a central x-frame. The columns' spigots can be seen, also jointed to the leg bearers. The shaped platform and frieze are not structural, but have a merely cosmetic role

The shaped platform, frieze and legs are veneered in mahogany, the columns are solid. The leg joint is a substantial dovetail

Once the outside of the platform has been cleaned up, it can be veneered. This is straightforward enough. First crossband the sides to provide a degree of protection from feet which will inevitably kick against it, then veneer the top before drilling the holes for the columns' spigots. For accuracy's sake, mark these out through the holes already drilled in the runner frame.

LEGS

The legs are made from maple, for its strength, and join the platform – or more correctly, the platform's maple framework – by means of a large dovetail. This joint is about as stressed as a dovetail can be, so make it as big as possible and a perfect fit.

The dovetails should be formed on the legs before they are profiled; make an oblique cut on the stock, then use this as a reference when cutting the long dovetail. This can be formed on the router table in the same way as the dovetail slips, if a large enough cutter is available. To create the shoulder above the dovetail, simply glue on a piece at the top of the leg.

THICKNESSER TAPERING JIG

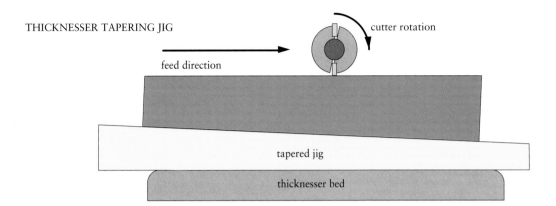

cutter rotation

feed direction

tapered jig

thicknesser bed

to achieve a symmetrical taper two jigs are required. In this example the first is at 3°, and the material is turned over to be tapered on the second at 6°. This gives an even 3° taper on each side

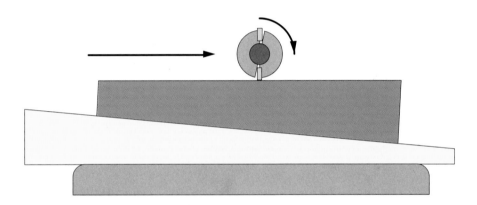

Working from a template indexed from the dovetail shoulder, mark out and bandsaw the profile of the leg. The resultant shape can be cleaned up either by hand, with disc and drum sanders, or by using a long profile cutter in a router table, with its bearing guided by the template. I normally favour the latter method which is, although quick and effective, a little hair-raising due to the reluctance of maple's end grain to be routed. Remember that the legs will be veneered, though, so surface finish is not critical.

The visual bulk of the legs is mitigated by their being tapered towards the foot. This is easy to do with a tapered jig in a thickness planer or rather, two tapered jigs: if the first side is thicknessed while sitting on a jig tapered to 3°, the second face

will require support at 6° to give symmetry (see the illustration above).

Veneer the legs in mahogany, crossbanding their leading edges, then cut the castors' tenons prior to assembling the legs, platform and columns. There is a school of thought that favours French polishing these components before assembly – I leave the decision to you.

TABLE TOP

The top itself represents a large area, much of which is unrestrained. Consequently, it is prudent to use a stable, man-made board, lipped and veneered.

FITTING TABLE LEAVES

It is unlikely that each of the leaves in an extending table will be a perfect fit on all sides, so they must be clearly marked underneath with their respective position; 1, 2, etc. This alone will not prevent people from fitting them out of sequence, and enabling the insertion of only one specific leaf must also be planned. I get round this by setting five dowel positions for each side of the meeting edges, using different positionings of four biscuits and one dowel for each combination. By altering the position in which the dowel is fitted, only the leaf's intended partner can be fitted to it. This results in a set of leaves which will only fit together in the right way – and provides a little puzzle for the table's owner.

Prepare four pieces of MDF – for each fixed side of the top and two leaves – by applying a solid mahogany lipping to all edges. This lipping should be mitred at what will be the outer corners of the fixed table top, and continuous along what will be the moulded edges.

Whenever a lipping is used, a counter veneer under the face veneer is necessary in order to prevent the joint line telegraphing through the veneer when shrinkage of the lipping occurs. A synthetic fibre is most suitable for the counter veneer on this piece, due to the large area to be covered: synthetic fibres are available in large, blemish-free sheets, have no grain direction and present a smooth, homogenous and even-coloured surface.

This double veneering on the surface of the top must be matched on the underside of the top. Altogether, this makes for a very large area if you're using Scotch glue – not impossible, but certainly taxing. This is a case where discretion is the better part of valour and the use of a vacuum press, or sub-contracting the veneering of the top to a maker with a hot press, is recommended.

After veneering, radius the two outer corners of each fixed leaf. However, before any further trimming, plane the meeting edges and mount them on the outer runners of the pack. Check that they are exactly perpendicular to the runners and that tracking is consistent, then mark and fit locating dowels or biscuits to the meeting edges. When this is done, close the leaves and trim the sides. Next, plane the long edges of the loose leaves, then fit each one in turn (see panel above).

When you are happy with the fit of each leaf, set up the table with all the leaves in place, fit leaf catches to each, and use a router with a side fence to machine a thumb-moulding to the edge.

FRIEZE AND DRAWERS

Nice as a maple runner pack is, the closed table is intended to conceal its extendibility, so I fitted a solid mahogany frieze to its perimeter. Radius the outer corners of the corner posts and biscuit the long sections to

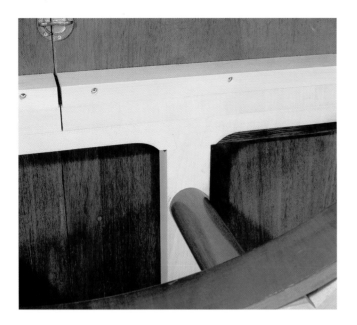

Simple frieze drawers are fitted to this table, but they can be omitted if not required. Like the frieze, the drawer front is crossbanded with mahogany veneer

The underside of the runners and table top when closed. Note the dovetail joint, and the clearance where the runners meet

these, then crossband the frieze with mahogany veneer. When the frieze is dry and has been cleaned up, biscuit it to the underside of the table top. Leave the ends which form the join between the two halves of the fixed table top a little proud at this stage, then trim them back with a block plane to a good mating fit.

This particular table displays two characteristics which could be viewed as departures from the norm, and which need not be incorporated unless specifically desired:

1 The leaves are not fitted with a frieze, as in this case the extra storage room required by leaves with friezes ruled it out.
2 Drawers are fitted to each end.

It is not usual for drawers to be included in a dining table, but there is room for them in this one due to the nature of the runners; as these are not linked with cross-members, a large space exists in the middle of each underframe which can easily accommodate a drawer.

The drawers are suspended from L-section runners which are screwed to the underside of the table top. Square-section runners, glued to the outer top of each drawer side, are located into these. The drawers are constructed to form an uninterrupted frieze when closed, so the side-to-front joints are long, sliding dovetails, the fronts overhang the drawer box sufficiently to hide the side hangings, and they are crossbanded. In all other respects the drawers are conventional in construction.

FINISHING

Mahogany polishes well with almost any hand-applied finish and is not hard to spray finish. Avoid plastic coatings though, as they will give a 'toffee apple' appearance. This example is French polished over an amber varnish base except for the top surface, which has a more durable, alcohol-resistant form of French polish.

An extending centre table in
mahogany, with a four-column
pedestal base

FIG 8.1
RUNNER PACK ASSEMBLY

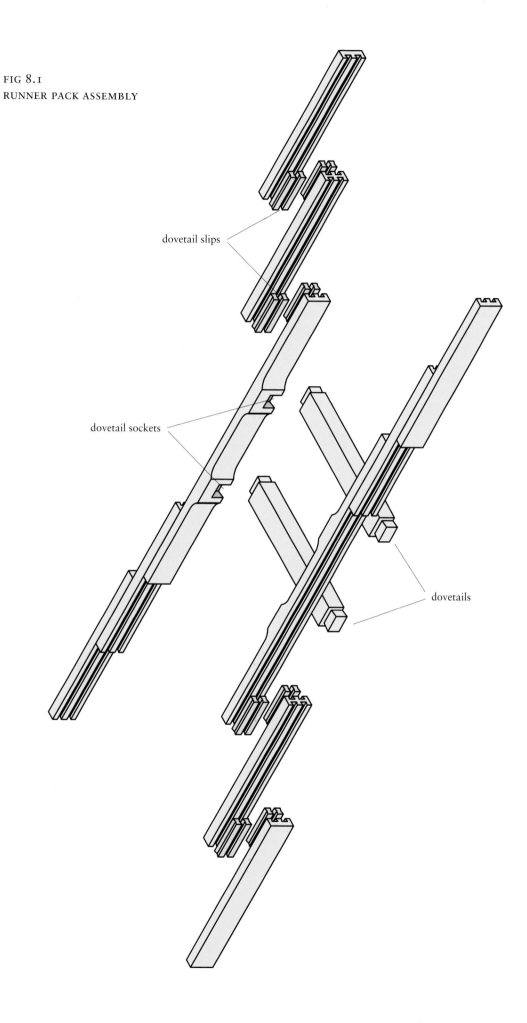

dovetail slips

dovetail sockets

dovetails

FIG 8.2 PRINCIPAL DIMENSIONS

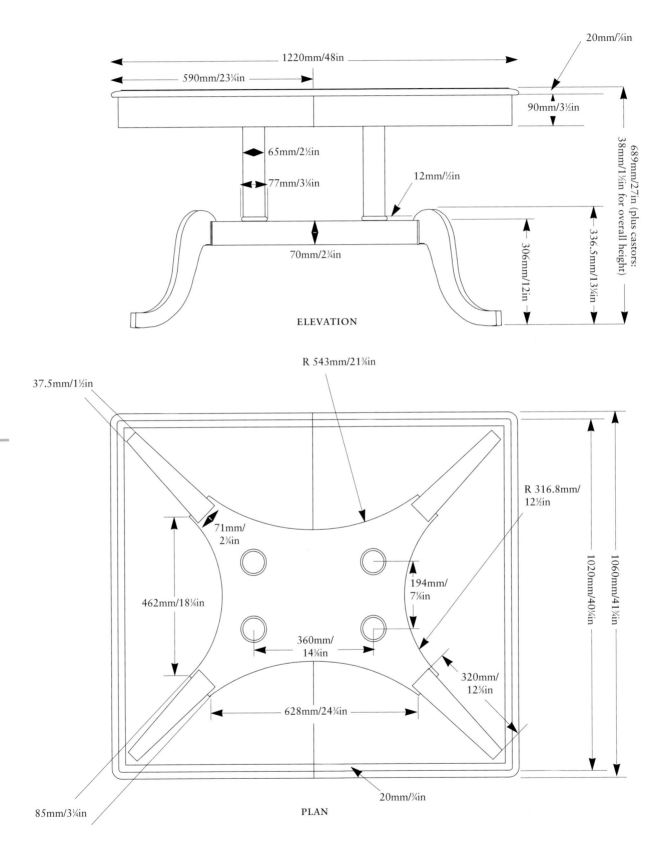

1220mm/48in

590mm/23¼in

20mm/⅞in

90mm/3½in

65mm/2½in

77mm/3⅛in

12mm/½in

689mm/27in (plus castors: 38mm/1½in for overall height)

336.5mm/13¼in

306mm/12in

70mm/2¾in

ELEVATION

R 543mm/21⅜in

37.5mm/1½in

R 316.8mm/ 12½in

71mm/ 2¾in

194mm/ 7⅝in

462mm/18⅛in

1060mm/41¾in

1020mm/40¼in

360mm/ 14⅛in

320mm/ 12⅝in

628mm/24¾in

20mm/¾in

85mm/3¼in

PLAN

FIG 8.3 STRETCHER AND COLUMNS

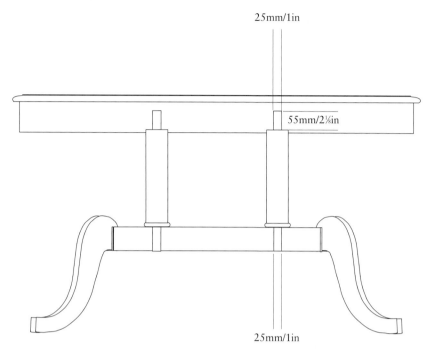

25mm/1in

55mm/2⅛in

25mm/1in

ELEVATION

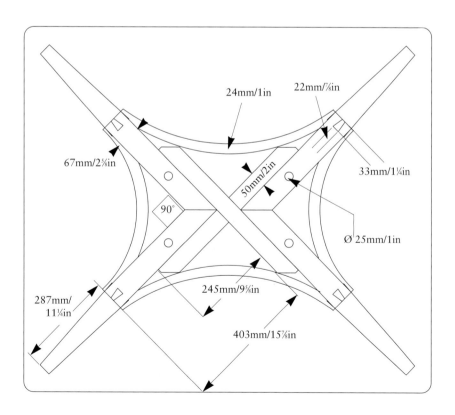

24mm/1in

22mm/⅞in

67mm/2⅝in

33mm/1¼in

50mm/2in

90°

Ø 25mm/1in

287mm/
11¼in

245mm/9⅝in

403mm/15⅞in

PLAN

FIG 8.4 PLAN VIEW SHOWING RUNNERS AND FIXED LEAVES

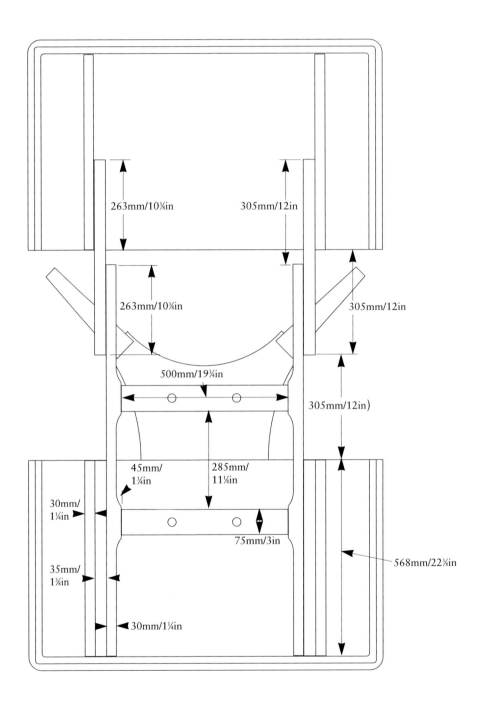

263mm/10⅜in

305mm/12in

263mm/10⅜in

305mm/12in

500mm/19¾in

305mm/12in)

45mm/
1¾in

285mm/
11¼in

30mm/
1¼in

75mm/3in

568mm/22⅜in

35mm/
1⅜in

30mm/1¼in

FIG 8.5 COLUMN HEIGHT

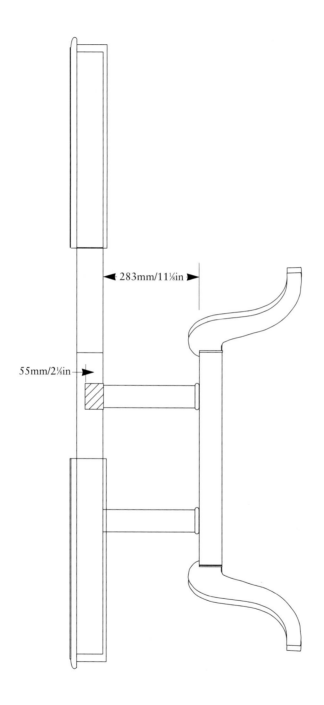

283mm/11⅛in

55mm/2⅛in

FIG 8.6 RUNNER PACK: DETAIL

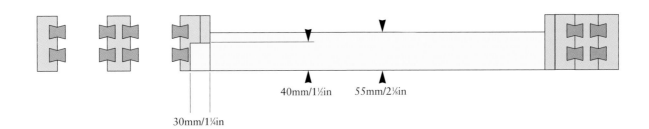

30mm/1¼in

40mm/1½in   55mm/2⅛in

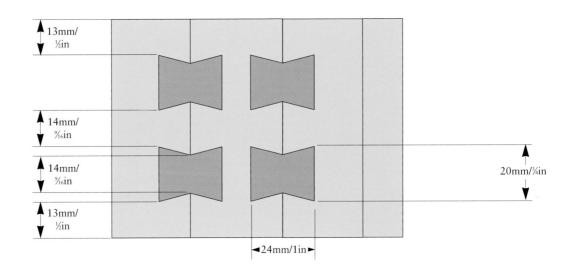

13mm/
½in

14mm/
⁹⁄₁₆in

14mm/
⁹⁄₁₆in

13mm/
½in

24mm/1in

20mm/¾in

FIG 8.7 RUNNER PACK: PARTIALLY EXPLODED PLAN VIEW

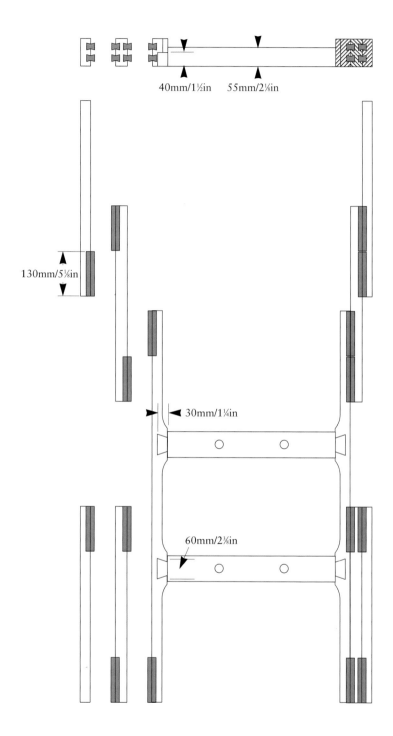

40mm/1½in   55mm/2⅛in

130mm/5⅛in

30mm/1¼in

60mm/2⅜in

I. Hall.

chapter nine

BREAKFRONT BOOKCASE

SPECIAL FEATURES

Sub-assemblies in furniture construction

Cornice mouldings

Enduringly popular – for more than 300 years – due to its prodigious storage capacity, the breakfront bookcase is an impressive form. To achieve their requisite imposing size while remaining manageable, such bookcases are constructed as a set of sub-assemblies and embellished with generous cornice mouldings and pediments, proportioned according to classical architectural conventions.

This form is enduringly popular
for its prodigious and versatile
storage capability. Alternative
arrangements include doors, or a
combination of doors and
drawers, to the base, and glazed
doors to the top section. The
broken pediment is a grandiose
flourish that may be omitted for
a more modest appearance

If there is a staple in the traditional cabinetmaker's diet, it is the breakfront bookcase. The
first examples of this form appeared some 300
years ago and they have been made continuously
ever since: people will always need storage
furniture and the breakfront bookcase is a
versatile solution to all kinds of storage problems.

This example is not untypical of the breed, having
the classical broken pediment at the top and definite
eighteenth-century bracket feet at the bottom,
although drawers are perhaps less usual in the base
than cupboard doors. If cupboard doors were fitted,
the base would need to be taller.

Another deviation from the norm, emphasizing
the flexibility of the basic design, is that the lower
pairs of what appear to be banks of three drawers
in each wing are in fact single, deep drawers, one
of which is fitted to hold bottles.

Many such pieces feature glazed doors in the upper
structure. The original purpose of these was to
protect valuable books – and most books in the
eighteenth century were valuable – from the

deleterious effects of soot from open fires. Such
doors often featured complex patterns of glazing
bars, decorative certainly, but again with a
practical purpose – large pieces of glass were
difficult and expensive to make at that time and
glazing bars broke up the doors into smaller areas.

Neither doors nor bars feature in this piece of
furniture, however, as its upper structure is intended
for the unobstructed display of glass and ceramics
rather than books.

As for the originals, a combination of solid and
veneered components are used, however, whereas
our Georgian predecessor would veneer onto clear
Baltic pine, I used MDF for this piece.

Another departure is that biscuit joints are used
extensively for the carcass joints. It is sometimes
imagined that craftsmen in the 'golden age'
dovetailed everything in sight; this is not the case,
as any restorer will testify. I have seen carcasses of
this type that are housed and rebated, others which
rely heavily on cut nails and glue, and Victorian
work using dowels, so biscuits are quite acceptable.

Glazed doors are often fitted to the top section; these protected books from soot when open fires provided heating. A practical solution to the high cost of large pieces of glass in Georgian times, the use of glazing bars presents an opportunity for decorative work

SUB-ASSEMBLIES

Despite their imposing size, these bookcases are nothing more than a collection of square carcasses, albeit with some decoration, and if each sub-assembly is viewed separately, then the project is less daunting. Convenient sub-divisions are:

- *base carcass;*
- *drawers;*
- *top carcass; and pediment.*

BASE CARCASS

The top of the base will receive a moulding and is an important structural component, so it has been made from joined boards of solid mahogany; all other carcass components are mahogany-lipped and -veneered MDF. Time spent drawing out a full-size plan or rod will be repaid later, as some of the relationships of the parts are not immediately obvious.

Cut the top and bottom of the base to their plan shapes, with the breakfront (see Fig 9.3), then rebate the top, bottom and sides to take the back panel.

Cut the vertical divisions to fit between the top and bottom and inside the back panel. Note that a solid mahogany facing is planted on to the front edges of these components, so they must be cut to the internal depth of the carcass less the thickness of these facings. They are notched at the front so that they present a full-height appearance where they form the side of the breakfront.

Now we come to the only mildly complicated part – the drawer runners and rails. These are simple frames, morticed and tenoned from oak, with mahogany front rails. They are biscuited between the

vertical components, two in the central breakfront and one in each wing. Once made, the two centre frames must be notched around the facings mentioned above, as must the carcass base, to give the carcass' front the appearance of a flush framework. This notching is best done by scribing round the ends of the facings with a marking knife, then cutting by hand, as gaps would give the game away.

Next, one last provision must be made for the running of the drawers. The bottom drawer in the centre of the base runs directly on the carcass floor: as this is a mahogany veneer over MDF, the drawer's oak sides would soon wear into it, causing all kinds of problems. All this trouble can be avoided by routing a housing of around 5mm (³⁄₁₆in) in depth where each drawer side will run, and inlaying a strip of oak into each of these.

From the illustrations you will see that a single, narrow facing is applied to the outer face of each vertical division as a dummy carcass member for the wing apertures. This is needed not only for visual effect, but also to provide clearance for the wings' drawers. It is merely a strip of solid mahogany biscuited to the division. The wings' drawer runner frames must be notched as for the two centre frames above.

The centre section of the base accommodates three graduated drawers. The runners and front rails are mortice-and-tenoned frames biscuited in position; note the oak bearing strips inlaid in the carcass floor to take the load of the bottom drawer. The usual drawer kickers are glued to the runners

With the exception of the frames, which are morticed and tenoned, all the carcass joints are biscuited. Examination of Fig 9.3 will reveal some unusual aspects to the way the parts fit together though, occasioned by the need for the carcass top to be uninterrupted. This conflicts with the requirement for the sides to be fitted outside the base, and then of course the drawer frames must be in place before the top and bottom are brought together. . .

All of this makes for a good exercise in planning a glue-up. First assemble the centre drawer frames and divisions, then slot the divisions into the bottom. Next, add one side and its mating runner frame, then the other. Now all of the remaining joints are in one orientation, uppermost, the top can be dropped on and clamps applied. Be sure to check for square. When dry, fit kickers to the drawer runners, and finally, screw the back panel into its rebate.

If this seems daunting and you are working alone, the divisions and centre runner packs can be glued up separately in advance, but again, make sure they are square or they may distort the whole carcass.

FEET AND MOULDINGS

The base carcass is supported on bracket feet, and to achieve the necessary offset in the vertical lines of feet and carcass, a base moulding is used.

Due to the weight that will eventually bear on this moulding when the piece is *in situ* and loaded with books and so on, a stuck moulding might prove inadequate. Consequently, for this piece, an ovolo moulding is routed on the edge of 50 x 22mm (2 x ⅞in) mahogany stock, which is then fixed under the perimeter edge of the carcass bottom. This means that the load runs straight through the carcass sides and divisions, moulding and feet, the latter being glued under the base moulding (see the mule chest in Chapter 5, page 75).

The moulding to the top of the base carcass is routed into the edge of the top member. Almost all of this moulding can be done using a bearing-guided router cutter running on the edge of the top itself, but the two internal corners of the breakfront will be left rounded by the cutter and must be finished off by hand. This procedure is fundamentally the same as that used to cut the internal mitres of the broken-arch door panels for the mule chest (see Chapter 5, page 82), but is

Bracket feet are glue-blocked to the underside of a base moulding, which is, in turn, fixed below the carcass to provide a secure mounting

The top member of the base carcass is solid mahogany, featuring an ovolo moulding to its perimeter. Most of this can be routed, but the internal mitres must be completed by hand

Drawers are made with solid
mahogany fronts, oak linings
and solid bottoms fitted in slips

The shallow drawer: note the
brass rod supporting the
top of the drawer front

somewhat easier due both to the shape and the material
used. Mahogany offers less resistance, but don't let
this lead you into going too far; work back in increments until an accurate mitre has been formed.

DRAWERS

The conventional drawers (those fitted to the central
aperture and the top drawers of the wings) are made
as already described – they have mahogany fronts
with oak sides and bottoms.

Both deep drawers in the wings are fitted with metal,
full-extension runners to allow them to be fully drawn
out of the carcass. The fronts of both are contrived
to look like two graduated drawers, matching those in
the central section. They are made up from three
pieces; two for the dummy drawer fronts, separated
by another the thickness of the drawer rails. These
parts are biscuited together and then, to complete the
illusion, a shallow groove is routed along the joins
with a 1.6mm (1⁄16in) cutter (see the photos here
and on page 162).

The drawer boxes are independent of the fronts,
which are screwed to them, giving considerable
freedom as regards their design and construction.

The requirement here was for one drawer fitted to
accommodate bottles and another to provide storage
for rolled papers.

The first of these is a simple, biscuited mahogany
box in which cross-pieces are housed. Compartments
are created with brass rods passing through the front,
cross-pieces and back; leave the assembly of this
arrangement until the box is polished to avoid the
difficulties caused by restricted access. As this drawer
box is so shallow, support for the top of the drawer
front is provided by braces made from brass rod.

The second drawer box is a biscuited oak box, with
scalloped sides.

TOP CARCASS

This is another veneered MDF box, with biscuit
joints used throughout. Again, the vertical components
must present an uninterrupted appearance, so the
sides are biscuited to the edges of the top and bottom,
and the divisions are notched where they oversail
at the breakfront.

Apply solid mahogany vertical facings to the leading
edges of the divisions, as for the base, and add

The scalloped sides of the second drawer. Note the construction of the false drawer fronts: a dummy rail is biscuited between fronts which match the real graduated drawers in the centre section. To enhance the illusion a groove is routed along the joins

a frieze to the top of the apertures. Plan the order of assembly of these solid parts carefully, as the frieze is biscuited back into the carcass and sideways into the facings – you will see that the facings and frieze must be presented to the carcass at the same time.

Both the veneered and the glass shelves are adjustable, being supported by brass pegs which locate in 5mm (³⁄₁₆in) holes drilled directly into the carcass sides (see Chapter 5, page 88). This is the least obtrusive system and works well in most situations. Pegs with soft rubber ends are available for use with glass shelves, but it is as effective to slide short sections of neoprene hose onto standard brass pegs.

CORNICE

For ease of transportation and handling, the cornice and pediment are both separate assemblies, fixed to the top carcass only when it is in place, and removable should the need arise.

The cornice is built around a framework, the visible sides of which are made of 22mm (⅞in) mahogany on edge. To this, the mouldings which

go to make up the cornice are applied (see Fig 9.2). The unseen part of the framework need not be particularly well finished; on period examples this component varies from the crisp to the agricultural, and gives a revealing insight into the attitude of the maker.

It is worth noting that all of the mouldings involved were produced using a ½in collet, 1800W router mounted on an inversion table. Only one non-standard cutter was used (for the large ogee) and then only because it was to hand; several standard examples feature in cutter suppliers' catalogues which would do just as well. Certainly, I felt no need of a spindle moulder even for this size of cornice, and I maintain that most furniture projects are well within the scope of the portable router.

When making up the mouldings, work from stock prepared accurately and cross-cut the pieces to convenient lengths before routing. This will ensure an easy passage through the cutter and consequently, smooth, consistent mouldings which require little hand finishing.

Considerable variety in the treatment of pediments will be found; this is one alternative from a bureau bookcase, made some time before the breakfront featured here. Note that the pediment oversails the side of the cornice; such variations make a considerable difference to the visual proportions and, therefore, to the 'feel' of the piece

As usual, err on the side of restraint when choosing mouldings. Only two simple patterns are used for this cornice, a cove and an ogee, which is quite complicated enough given the other visual elements (the breakfront, the pediment and so on). It is all too easy to overdo it, resulting in a wedding cake effect.

Accurate mitring is important, and best done using a mitre guillotine. Each layer is mitred round the framework individually, cove first, then ogee.

PEDIMENT

The pediment is made up from the same mouldings as the cornice, supplemented with an additional ovolo mould between the large ogee and the cove. This adds visual weight and importance to these relatively short sections. It will be seen from the photographs that the mouldings are mitred and returned at both ends: those at the centre return just far enough to cover the ends of the mouldings while the outer returns extend as far as is needed to prevent their ends being visible when the piece is assembled and sited. These mouldings are fixed to a shaped piece of mahogany which provides the necessary angles. Here it is essential to work from an accurate drawing, as the shape of the kite, its angles, and the size and position of the scalloped central detail defines the shape of the pediment itself: the pediment must conform to classical proportions or it will be no more than a pastiche.

Experiment with different shapes and refer to photographs of period work to ensure correctness. You will find many variations on the treatment of the central detail; sometimes an urn-shaped finial sits on a small plinth between the scallops, sometimes there is only one large scallop. For this piece two scallops are used, but with a plain moulding mitred around the flat at their junction.

In keeping with the rest of the bookcase's construction, the pediment is assembled with biscuit joints.

ASSEMBLY

After polishing, by whatever means chosen, and delivery – which for a piece of this size is no mean

feat – the bookcase should be assembled in its final position. On no account should it be moved once assembled.

Sit the base carcass in place, then add the top carcass, screwing the two together from the underside of the base's top. Fit the cornice and pediment, then slide the drawers into the carcass and add the shelves. Note that if the carcass is sitting on an uneven floor, the weight of the assembly will cause it to distort. This will be revealed by uneven gaps around the drawers, and in extreme cases may cause the drawers to jam altogether.

To correct any distortion in the bookcase, place shims under the feet until all is well, ensuring that all the feet are firmly in contact with the floor. When installing furniture of this kind, I take along a good selection of shims of different thicknesses, from veneer to small offcuts of MDF.

The bookcase pictured was, as mentioned earlier, intended to display glass and ceramics. A dark background is not ideal for this, so I added a false back panel made from 6mm (¼in) MDF covered in light-coloured cloth. This is held in place with self-adhesive Velcro.

Fɪɢ 9.ɪ ɢᴇɴᴇʀᴀʟ ᴀʀʀᴀɴɢᴇᴍᴇɴᴛ

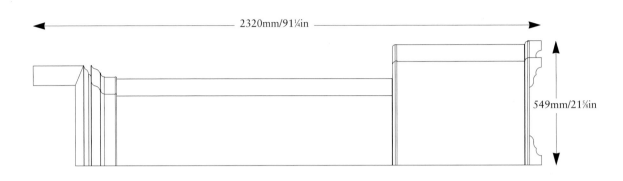

2320mm/91¼in

549mm/21⅝in

LEFT ELEVATION

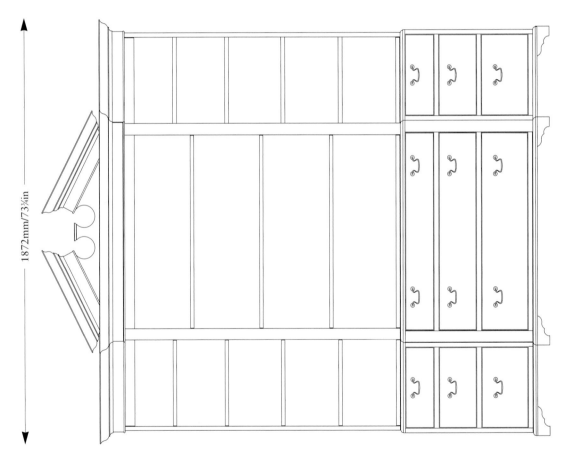

1872mm/73¾in

FRONT ELEVATION

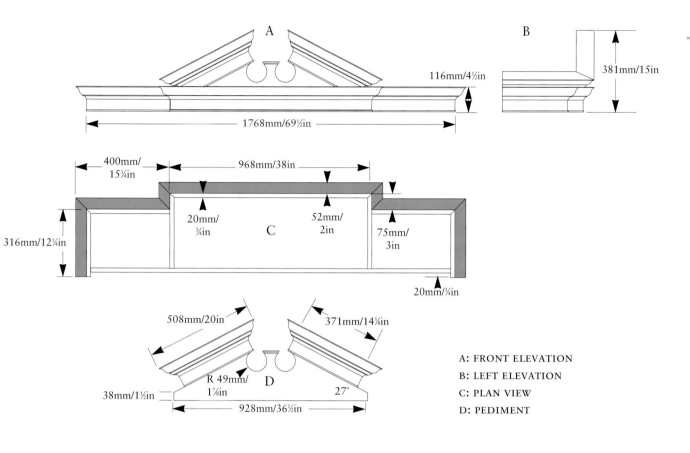

A: FRONT ELEVATION
B: LEFT ELEVATION
C: PLAN VIEW
D: PEDIMENT

116mm/4½in

1768mm/69½in

381mm/15in

400mm/15¾in

968mm/38in

316mm/12¼in

20mm/¾in

52mm/2in

C

75mm/3in

20mm/¾in

508mm/20in

371mm/14⅝in

R 49mm/1⅞in

D

27°

38mm/1½in

928mm/36½in

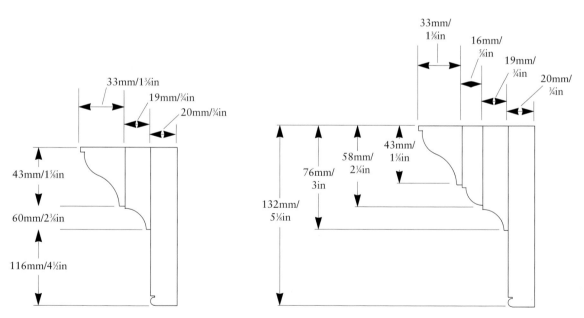

33mm/1⅜in

19mm/¾in

20mm/¾in

43mm/1⅝in

60mm/2⅜in

116mm/4½in

33mm/1⅜in

16mm/⅝in

19mm/¾in

20mm/¾in

76mm/3in

58mm/2¼in

43mm/1⅝in

132mm/5⅛in

FIG 9.2 CORNICE AND MOULDING DETAIL

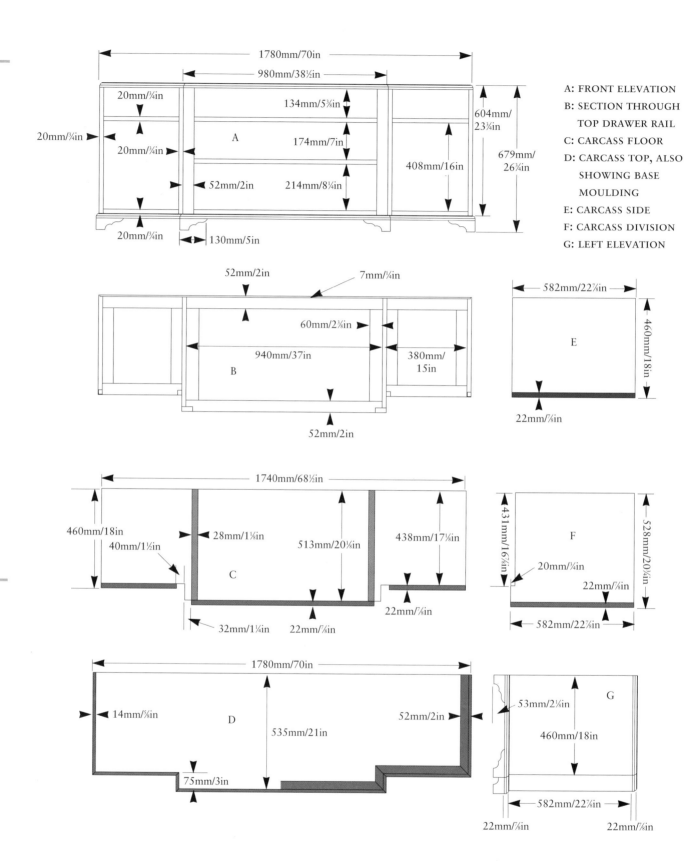

A: FRONT ELEVATION
B: SECTION THROUGH
   TOP DRAWER RAIL
C: CARCASS FLOOR
D: CARCASS TOP, ALSO
   SHOWING BASE
   MOULDING
E: CARCASS SIDE
F: CARCASS DIVISION
G: LEFT ELEVATION

FIG 9.3 BASE CARCASS: PLANS AND ELEVATIONS

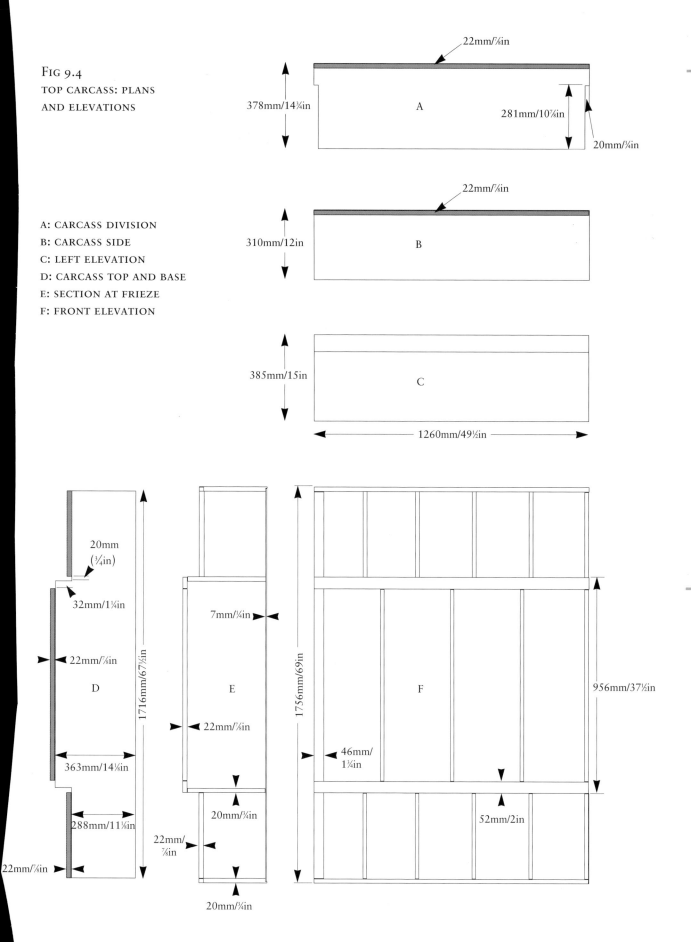

FIG 9.4
TOP CARCASS: PLANS
AND ELEVATIONS

A: CARCASS DIVISION
B: CARCASS SIDE
C: LEFT ELEVATION
D: CARCASS TOP AND BASE
E: SECTION AT FRIEZE
F: FRONT ELEVATION

22mm/⅞in

378mm/14¾in

A

281mm/10⅞in

20mm/¾in

22mm/⅞in

310mm/12in

B

385mm/15in

C

1260mm/49½in

20mm
(¾in)

32mm/1¼in

22mm/⅞in

D

1716mm/67½in

363mm/14⅛in

288mm/11⅛in

22mm/⅞in

7mm/¼in

E

22mm/⅞in

20mm/¾in

22mm/
⅞in

20mm/¾in

1756mm/69in

F

46mm/
1¾in

52mm/2in

956mm/37½in

ABOUT THE AUTHOR

Paul Richardson has had an eclectic career, based around a core of practical work. On leaving school he became an apprentice jeweller in his native town of Lincoln, later setting up on his own, making jewellery and other items in precious metals.

His interest in music led him to turn his attention to the construction of stringed instruments, learning the craft from a violin-maker. He opened his own guitar workshop and became maker, consultant and technician to a number of international recording artists, sometimes accompanying them on the road.

From here he moved to cabinetmaking, becoming the fifth-generation of his family to follow this path – documentation shows that his forebears arrived in England from France in the early nineteenth century, basing themselves in Manchester where they soon established a furniture-making business. It was here that Paul's grandfather trained as a French polisher.

Paul has had no formal training in cabinetmaking, learning his techniques through the oral tradition. His approach bears testimony to this method. He has worked with interior designers and restorers, and has specialized in accurate copies of Georgian furniture. He set up his own furniture-making and restoration workshop in Sussex, taking commissions from local clients.

Paul enjoys writing and worked for a number of years as a freelance journalist across a range of magazine titles, including music, computing and woodworking, during his years as a maker.

In the early 1990s he discovered the world of the Apple Mac which was to change the course of his career, leading him to explore design, graphics, and multi-media, finally taking the leap into full-time publishing when he became editor of *The Woodworker* in 1995.

A year later he joined GMC Publications, launching the innovative *Furniture & Cabinetmaking* – it is now the leading magazine in its field. Paul became Managing Editor of the Magazines Division of GMC in the spring of 1998.

He lives with his wife and two children in rural Sussex and pursues his interest in photography and music.

INDEX

WOODWORKING

Bird Boxes and Feeders for the Garden	*Dave Mackenzie*
Complete Woodfinishing	*Ian Hosker*
David Charlesworth's Furniture-Making Techniques	*David Charlesworth*
Furniture & Cabinetmaking Projects	*GMC Publications*
Furniture-Making Projects for the Wood Craftsman	*GMC Publications*
Furniture-Making Techniques for the Wood Craftsman	*GMC Publications*
Furniture Projects	*Rod Wales*
Furniture Restoration (Practical Crafts)	*Kevin Jan Bonner*
Furniture Restoration and Repair for Beginners	*Kevin Jan Bonner*
Furniture Restoration Workshop	*Kevin Jan Bonner*
Green Woodwork	*Mike Abbott*
Making & Modifying Woodworking Tools	*Jim Kingshott*
Making Chairs and Tables	*GMC Publications*
Making Classic English Furniture	*Paul Richardson*
Making Fine Furniture	*Tom Darby*
Making Little Boxes from Wood	*John Bennett*
Making Shaker Furniture	*Barry Jackson*
Making Woodwork Aids and Devices	*Robert Wearing*
Minidrill: Fifteen Projects	*John Everett*
Pine Furniture Projects for the Home	*Dave Macken…*
Router Magic: Jigs, Fixtures and Tricks to Unleash your Router's Full Potential	*Bill Hylt…*
Routing for Beginners	*Anthony Bai…*
Scrollsaw Pattern Book	*John Ever…*
The Scrollsaw: Twenty Projects	*John Ever…*
Sharpening: The Complete Guide	*Jim Kingsh…*
Sharpening Pocket Reference Book	*Jim Kingsh…*
Space-Saving Furniture Projects	*Dave Macken…*
Stickmaking: A Complete Course	*Andrew Jones & Clive Geor…*
Stickmaking Handbook	*Andrew Jones & Clive Geor…*
Test Reports: *The Router* and *Furniture & Cabinetmaking*	*GMC Publicatio…*
Veneering: A Complete Course	*Ian Hosk…*
Woodfinishing Handbook (Practical Crafts)	*Ian Hosk…*
Woodworking with the Router: Professional Router Techniques any Woodworker can Use	*Bill Hylton & Fred Matla…*
The Workshop	*Jim Kingsh…*

WOODTURNING

Adventures in Woodturning	*David Springett*
Bert Marsh: Woodturner	*Bert Marsh*
Bill Jones' Notes from the Turning Shop	*Bill Jones*
Bill Jones' Further Notes from the Turning Shop	*Bill Jones*
Bowl Turning Techniques Masterclass	*Tony Boase*
Colouring Techniques for Woodturners	*Jan Sanders*
The Craftsman Woodturner	*Peter Child*
Decorative Techniques for Woodturners	*Hilary Bowen*
Faceplate Turning	*GMC Publications*
Fun at the Lathe	*R.C. Bell*
Further Useful Tips for Woodturners	*GMC Publications*
Illustrated Woodturning Techniques	*John Hunnex*
Intermediate Woodturning Projects	*GMC Publications*
Keith Rowley's Woodturning Projects	*Keith Rowley*
Multi-Centre Woodturning	*Ray Hopper*
Practical Tips for Turners & Carvers	*GMC Publications*
Spindle Turning	*GMC Publications*
Turning Green Wood	*Michael O'Donnell*
Turning Miniatures in Wood	*John Sainsbu…*
Turning Pens and Pencils	*Kip Christensen & Rex Burningha…*
Turning Wooden Toys	*Terry Lawren…*
Understanding Woodturning	*Ann & Bob Philli…*
Useful Techniques for Woodturners	*GMC Publicatio…*
Useful Woodturning Projects	*GMC Publicatio…*
Woodturning: Bowls, Platters, Hollow Forms, Vases, Vessels, Bottles, Flasks, Tankards, Plates	*GMC Publicatio…*
Woodturning: A Foundation Course (New Edition)	*Keith Rowl…*
Woodturning: A Fresh Approach	*Robert Chapm…*
Woodturning: An Individual Approach	*Dave Reges…*
Woodturning: A Source Book of Shapes	*John Hunn…*
Woodturning Jewellery	*Hilary Bow…*
Woodturning Masterclass	*Tony Boa…*
Woodturning Techniques	*GMC Publicatio…*
Woodturning Tools & Equipment Test Reports	*GMC Publicatio…*
Woodturning Wizardry	*David Spring…*

WOODCARVING

The Art of the Woodcarver	*GMC Publications*
Carving Architectural Detail in Wood: The Classical Tradition	*Frederick Wilbur*
Carving Birds & Beasts	*GMC Publications*
Carving Nature: Wildlife Studies in Wood	*Frank Fox-Wilson*
Carving on Turning	*Chris Pye*
Carving Realistic Birds	*David Tippey*
Decorative Woodcarving	*Jeremy Williams*
Elements of Woodcarving	*Chris Pye*
Essential Tips for Woodcarvers	*GMC Publications*
Essential Woodcarving Techniques	*Dick Onians*
Further Useful Tips for Woodcarvers	*GMC Publications*
Lettercarving in Wood: A Practical Course	*Chris Pye*
Making & Using Working Drawings for Realistic Model Animals	*Basil Fordham*
Power Tools for Woodcarving	*David Tippe…*
Practical Tips for Turners & Carvers	*GMC Publication…*
Relief Carving in Wood: A Practical Introduction	*Chris Py…*
Understanding Woodcarving	*GMC Publications…*
Understanding Woodcarving in the Round	*GMC Publications…*
Useful Techniques for Woodcarvers	*GMC Publications…*
Wildfowl Carving – Volume 1	*Jim Pearce…*
Wildfowl Carving – Volume 2	*Jim Pearce…*
The Woodcarvers	*GMC Publications…*
Woodcarving: A Complete Course	*Ron Butterfield…*
Woodcarving: A Foundation Course	*Zoë Gertner…*
Woodcarving for Beginners	*GMC Publications…*
Woodcarving Tools & Equipment Test Reports	*GMC Publications…*
Woodcarving Tools, Materials & Equipment	*Chris Pye…*

VIDEOS

Drop-in and Pinstuffed Seats	*David James*	Twists and Advanced Turning	*Dennis Whit*
Stuffover Upholstery	*David James*	Sharpening the Professional Way	*Jim Kingsho*
Elliptical Turning	*David Springett*	Sharpening Turning & Carving Tools	*Jim Kingsho*
Woodturning Wizardry	*David Springett*	Bowl Turning	*John Jord*
Turning Between Centres: The Basics	*Dennis White*	Hollow Turning	*John Jord*
Turning Bowls	*Dennis White*	Woodturning: A Foundation Course	*Keith Rowl*
Boxes, Goblets and Screw Threads	*Dennis White*	Carving a Figure: The Female Form	*Ray Gonzal*
Novelties and Projects	*Dennis White*	The Router: A Beginner's Guide	*Alan Goods*
Classic Profiles	*Dennis White*	The Scroll Saw: A Beginner's Guide	*John Bur*

MAGAZINES

WOODTURNING ◆ WOODCARVING ◆ FURNITURE & CABINETMAKING ◆ THE ROUTER
THE DOLLS' HOUSE MAGAZINE ◆ BUSINESSMATTERS ◆ WATER GARDENING
EXOTIC GARDENING ◆ OUTDOOR PHOTOGRAPHY ◆ WOODWORKING

The above represents a full list of all titles currently published or scheduled to be published.
All are available direct from the Publishers or through bookshops, newsagents and specialist retailers.
To place an order, or to obtain a complete catalogue, contact:

GMC Publications,
Castle Place, 166 High Street, Lewes, East Sussex BN7 1XU, United Kingdom
Tel: 01273 488005 Fax: 01273 478606
E-mail: pubs@thegmcgroup.com

Orders by credit card are accepted